Clarel by Herman Melville

Part II – (of IV) The Wilderness

Herman Melville was born in New York City on August 1st, 1819, the third of eight children.

At the age of 7 Melville contracted scarlet fever which was to permanently diminish his eyesight. At this time Melville was described as being "very backwards in speech and somewhat slow in comprehension."

His father died when he was 12 leaving the family in very straitened times. Just 14 Melville took a job in a bank paying $150 a year that he obtained via his uncle, Peter Gansevoort, who was one of the directors of the New York State Bank.

After a failed stint as a surveyor he signed on to go to sea and travelled across the Atlantic to Liverpool and then on further voyages to the Pacific on adventures which would soon become the architecture of his novels. Whilst travelling he joined a mutiny, was jailed, fell in love with a South Pacific beauty and became known as a figure of opposition to the coercion of native Hawaiians to the Christian religion.

He drew from these experiences in his books Typee, Omoo, and White-Jacket. These were published as novels, the first initially in London in 1846.

By 1851 his masterpiece, Moby Dick, was ready to be published. It is perhaps, and certainly at the time, one of the most ambitious novels ever written. However, it never sold out its initial print run of 3,000 and Melville's earnings on this masterpiece were a mere $556.37.

In succeeding years his reputation waned and he found life increasingly difficult. His family was growing, now four children, and a stable income was essential.

With his finances in a disappointing state Melville took the advice of friends that a change in career was called for. For many others public lecturing had proved very rewarding. From late 1857 to 1860, Melville embarked upon three lecture tours, where he spoke mainly on Roman statuary and sightseeing in Rome.

In 1876 he was at last able to publish privately his 16,000 line epic poem Clarel. It was to no avail. The book had an initial printing of 350 copies, but sales failed miserably.

On December 31st, 1885 Melville was at last able to retire. His wife had inherited several small legacies and provide them with a reasonable income.

Herman Melville, novelist, poet, short story writer and essayist, died at his home on September 28rh 1891 from cardiovascular disease.

Index of Contents

Canto I - The Cavalcade
A down the Dolorosa Lane
The mounted pilgrims file in train
Whose clatter jars each open space;

Then, muffled in, shares change apace
As, striking sparks in vaulted street,
Clink, as in cave, the horses' feet.
Not from brave Chaucer's Tabard Inn
They pictured wend; scarce shall they win
Fair Kent, and Canterbury ken;
Nor franklin, squire, nor morris-dance
Of wit and story good as then:
Another age, and other men,
And life an unfulfilled romance.

First went the turban—guide and guard
In escort armed and desert trim;
The pilgrims next: whom now to limn.
One there the light rein slackly drew,
And skimming glanced, dejected never—
While yet the pilgrimage was new—
On sights ungladsome howsoever.
Cordial he turned his aspect clear
On all that passed; man, yea, and brute
Enheartening by a blithe salute,
Chirrup, or pat, in random cheer.
This pleasantness, which might endear,
Suffused was with a prosperous look
That bordered vanity, but took
Fair color as from ruddy heart.
A priest he was—though but in part;
For as the Templar old combined
The cavalier and monk in one;
In Derwent likewise might you find
The secular and cleric tone.
Imported or domestic mode,
Thought's last adopted style he showed;
Abreast kept with the age, the year,
And each bright optimistic mind,
Nor lagged with Solomon in rear,
And Job, the furthermost behind—
Brisk marching in time's drum-corps van
Abreast with whistlingJonathan.
Tho' English, with an English home,
His spirits through Creole cross derived
The light and effervescent foam;
And youth in years mature survived.
At saddle-bow a book was laid
Convenient—tinted in the page
Which did urbanely disengage
Sadness and doubt from all things sad
And dubious deemed. Confirmed he read:

A priest o' the club—a taking man,
And rather more than Lutheran.
A cloth cape, light in air afloat,
And easy set of cleric coat,
Seemed emblems of that facile wit,
Which suits the age—a happy fit.

Behind this good man's stirrups, rode
A solid stolid Elder, shod
With formidable boots. He went
Like Talus in a foundry cast;
Furrowed his face, with wrinkles massed.
He claimed no indirect descent
From Grampian kirk and covenant.
But recent sallying from home,
Late he assigned three days to Rome.
He saw the host go by. The crowd,
Made up from many a tribe and place
Of Christendom, kept seemly face:
Took off the hat, or kneeled, or bowed;
But he the helm rammed down apace:
Discourteous to the host, agree,
Tho' to a parting soul it went;
Nor deemed that, were it mummery,
'Twas pathos too. This hard dissent—
Transferred to Salem in remove,—
Led him to carp, and try disprove
Legend and site by square and line:
Aside time's violet mist he'd shove—
Quite disenchant the Land Divine.
So fierce he hurled zeal's javelin home,
It drove beyond the mark—pierced Rome,
And plunged beyond, thro' enemy
To friend. Scarce natural piety
Might live, abiding such a doom.
Traditions beautiful and old
Which with maternal arms enfold
Millions, else orphaned and made poor,
No plea could lure him to endure.
Concerned, meek Christian ill might bear
To mark this worthy brother rash,
Deeming he served religion there,
Work up the fag end of Voltaire,
And help along faith's final crash—
If that impend.
His fingers pressed
A ferule of black thorn: he bore
A pruning-knife in belt; in vest

A measuring-tape wound round a core;
And field-glass slung athwart the chest;
While peeped from holsters old and brown,
Horse-pistols—and they were his own.

A hale one followed, good to see,
English and Greek in pedigree;
Of middle-age; a ripe gallant,
A banker of the rich Levant;
In florid opulence preserved
Like peach in syrup. Ne'er he swerved
From morning bath, and dinner boon,
And velvet nap in afternoon,
And lounge in garden with cigar.
His home was Thessalonica,
Which views Olympus. But, may be,
Little he weened ofJove and gods
In synod mid those brave abodes;
Nor, haply, read or weighed Paul's plea
Addressed from Athens o'er the sea
Unto the Thessalonians old:
His bonds he scanned, and weighed his gold.
Parisian was his garb, and gay.
Upon his saddle-pommel lay
A rich Angora rug, for shawl
Or pillow, just as need might fall;
Not the Brazilian leopard's hair
Or toucan's plume may show more fair;
Yet, serving light convenience mere,
Proved but his heedless affluent cheer.
Chief exercise this sleek one took
Was toying with a tissue book
At intervals, and leaf by leaf
Gently reducing it. In brief,
With tempered yet Capuan zest,
Of cigarettes he smoked the best.
This wight did Lady Fortune love:
Day followed day in treasure-trove.
Nor only so, but he did run
In unmistrustful reveries bright

Beyond his own career to one
Who should continue it in light
Of lineal good times.
High walled,
An Eden owned he nigh his town,
Which locked in leafy emerald
A frescoed lodge. There Nubians armed,

Tall eunuchs virtuous in zeal,
In shining robes, with glittering steel,
Patrolled about his daughter charmed,
Inmost inclosed in nest of bowers,
By gorgons served, the dread she-powers,
Duennas: maiden more than fair:
How fairer in his rich conceit—
An Argive face, and English hair
Sunny as May in morning sweet:
A damsel for Apollo meet;
And yet a mortal's destined bride-
Bespoken, yes, affianced late
To one who by the senior's side
Rode rakishly deliberate—
A sprig of Smyrna, Glaucon he.
His father (such ere long to be)
Well loved him, nor that sole he felt
That fortune here had kindly dealt
Another court-card into hand—

The youth with gold at free command;—
No, but he also liked his clan,
His kinsmen, and his happy way;
And over wine would pleased repay
His parasites: Well may ye say
The boy's the bravest gentleman!—
From Beyrout late had come the pair
To further schemes of finance hid
And for a pasha's favor bid
And grave connivance. That affair
Yet lingered. So, dull time to kill,
They wandered, anywhere, at will.
Scarce through self-knowledge or self-love
They ventured Judah's wilds to rove,
As time, ere long, and place, may prove.

Came next in file three sumpter mules
With all things needful for the tent,
And panniers which the Greek o'errules;
For there, with store of nourishment,
Rosoglio pink and wine of gold
Slumbered as in the smugglers' hold.

Viewing those Levantines in way
Of the snared lion, which from grate
Marks the light throngs on holiday,
Nor e'er relaxes in his state
Of rigorous gloom; rode one whose air

Revealed—but, for the nonce, forbear.
Mortmain his name, or so in whim
Some moral wit had christened him.

Upon that creature men traduce
For patience under their abuse;
For whose requital there's assigned
No heaven; that thing of dreamful kind—
The ass—elected for the ease,
Good Nehemiah followed these;
His Bible under arm, and leaves
Of tracts still fluttering in sheaves.
In pure good will he bent his view
To right and left. The ass, pearl-gray,
Matched well the rider's garb in hue,
And sorted with the ashy way;
Upon her shoulders' jointed play
The white cross gleamed, which the untrue
Yet innocent fair legends say,
Memorializes Christ our Lord
When Him with palms the throngs adored
Upon the foal. Many a year
The wanderer's heart had longed to view
Green banks of Jordan dipped in dew;
Oft had he watched with starting tear
Pack-mule and camel, horse and spear,
Monks, soldiers, pilgrims, helm and hood,
The variegated annual train
In vernal Easter caravan,
Bound unto Gilgal's neighborhood.
Nor less belief his heart confessed
Not die he should till knees had pressed
The Palmers' Beach. Which trust proved true:
'Twas charity gave faith her due:
Without publicity or din
It was the student moved herein.

He, Clarel, with the earnest face
Which fitful took a hectic dye,
Kept near the saint. With equal pace
Came Rolfe in saddle pommeled high,
Yet e'en behind that peaked redoubt
Sat Indian-like, in pliant way,
As if he were an Osage scout,
Or Gaucho of the Paraguay.

Lagging in rear of all the train
As hardly he pertained thereto

Or his right place therein scarce knew,
Rode one who frequent turned again
To pore behind. He seemed to be
In reminiscence folded ever,
Or some deep moral fantasy;
At whiles in face a dusk and shiver,
As if in heart he heard amazed
The sighing of Ravenna's wood
Of pines, and saw the phantom knight
(Boccaccio's) with the dagger raised
Still hunt the lady in her flight
From solitude to solitude.
'Twas Vine. Nor less for day dream, still
The rein he held with lurking will.

So filed the muster whose array
hreaded the Dolorosa's way.

Canto II - The Skull Cap

"See him in his uncheerful head-piece!
Libertad's on the Mexic coin
Would better suit me for a shade-piece:
Ah, had I known he was to join!"—
So chid the Greek, the banker one
Perceiving Mortmain there at hand,
And in allusion to a dun
Skull-cap he wore. Derwent light reined
The steed; and thus: "Beg pardon now,
It looks a little queer, concede;
Nor less the cap fits well-shaped brow;
It yet may prove the wishing-cap
Of Fortunatus."
"No indeed,
No, no, for that had velvet nap
Of violet with silver tassel—
Much like my smoking-cap, you see,
Light laughed the Smyrniote, that vassal
Of health and young vivacity.
"Glaucon, be still," the senior said
(And yet he liked to hear him too);
"I say it doth but ill bestead
To have a black cap in our crew."
"Pink, pink," cried Glaucon, "pink's the hue:—
"Pink cap and ribbons of the pearl,
A Paradise of bodice,

The Queen of Sheba's laundry girl—
"Hallo, what now? They come to halt
Down here in glen! Well, well, we'll vault."
His song arrested, so he spake
And light dismounted, wide awake.—
"A sprightly comrade have you here,"
Said Derwent in the senior's ear.
The banker turned him: "Folly, folly—
But good against the melancholy."

Canto III - By the Garden

Sheep-tracks they'd look, at distance seen,
Did any herbage border them,
Those slender foot-paths slanting lean
Down or along waste slopes which hem
The high-lodged, walled Jerusalem.
Slipped from Bethesda's Pool leads one
Which by an arch across is thrown
Kedron the brook. The Virgin's Tomb
(Whence the near gate the Latins name—
St. Stephen's, as the Lutherans claim—
Hard by the place of martyrdom),
Time-worn in sculpture dim, is set
Humbly inearthed by Olivet.
'Tis hereabout now halt the band,
And by Gethsemane at hand,
For few omitted trifles wait
And guardsman whom adieus belate.
Some light dismount.
But hardly here,
Where on the verge they might foretaste
Or guess the flavor of the waste,
Greek sire and son took festive cheer.
Glaucon not less a topic found
At venture. One old tree becharmed
Leaned its decrepit trunk deformed
Over the garden's wayside bound:
"See now: this yellow olive wood
They carve in trinkets—rosary—rood:
Of these we must provide some few
For travel-gifts, ere we for good
Set out for home. And why not too
Some of those gems the nuns reverc
In hands of veteran venders here,
Wrought from the Kedron's saffron block

In the Monk's Glen, Mar Saba's rock;
And cameos of the Dead Sea stone?"
"Buy what ye will, be it Esau's flock,"
The other said: but for that stone—
Avoid, nor name!"
"That stone? what one?"
And cast a look of grieved surprise
Marking the senior's ruffled guise;
"Those cameos of Death's Sea—"
"Have done,
I beg! Unless all joy you'd cripple,
Both noun omit and participle."
"Dear sir, what noun? strange grammar's this."
"Have I expressed myself amiss?
Oh, don't you think it is but spleen:
A well-bred man counts it unclean
This name of—boy, and can't you guess?
Last bankruptcy without redress!"
"For heaven's sake!"
"With that ill word
Whose first is D and last is H,
No matter what be in regard,
Let none of mine ere crape his speech,
But shun it, ay, and shun the knell
Of each derivative."
"Oh, well—
I see, I see; with all my heart!
Each conjugation will I curb,
All moods and tenses of the verb;
And, for the noun, to save from errors
I'll use instead—the 'King of Terrors. ' "
"Sir, change the topic.—Would 'twere done,
This scheme of ours, and we clean gone
From out this same dull land so holy
Which breeds but blues and melancholy.
To while our waiting I thought good
To join these travelers on their road;
But there's a bird in saucy glee
Trills—Fool, retreat; 'tis not for thee.
Had I fair pretext now, I'd turn.
But yonder—he don't show concern,"
Glancing toward Derwent, lounging there
Holding his horse with easy air
Slack by the rein.
With morning zest,
In sound digestion unoppressed,
The clergyman's good spirits made
A Tivoli of that grim glade.

And turning now his cheery eyes
Toward Salem's towers in solemn guise
Stretched dumb along the Mount of God,
He cried to Clarel waiting near
In saddle-seat and gazing drear:
"A canter, lad, on steed clean-shod
Didst ever take on English sod?
The downs, the downs! Yet even here
For a fair matin ride withal
I like the run round yonder wall.
Hight have you, outlook; and the view
Varies as you the turn pursue."—
So he, thro' inobservance, blind
To that preoccupied young mind,
In frame how different, in sooth—
Pained and reverting still to Ruth
Immured and parted from him there
Behind those ramparts of despair.
Mortmain, whose wannish eyes declared
How ill thro' night-hours he had fared,
By chance overheard, and muttered—"Brass,
A sounding brass and tinkling cymbal!
Who he that with a tongue so nimble
Affects light heart in such a pass?"
And full his cloud on Derwent bent:
"Yea, and but thou seem'st well content.
But turn, another thing's to see:
Thy back's upon Gethsemane."
The priest wheeled short: What kind of man
Was this? The other re-began:
"'Tis Terra Santa—Holy Land:
Terra Damnata though's at hand
Within."—"You mean where Judas stood?
Yes, monks locate and name that ground;
They've railed it off. Good, very good:
It minds one of a vacant pound.—
We tarry long: why lags our man?"
And rose; anew glanced toward the hight.
Here Mortmain from the words and plight
Conjecture drew; and thus he ran:
"Be some who with the god will sup,
Happy to share his paschal wine.
'Tis well. But the ensuing cup,
The bitter cup?"
"Art a divine?"
Asked Derwent, turning that aside;
"Methinks, good friend, too much you chide.
I know these precincts. Still, believe—

And let's discard each idle trope—
Rightly considered, they can give
A hope to man, a cheerful hope."
"Not for this world. The Christian plea—
What basis has it, but that here
Man is not happy, nor can be?
There it confirms philosophy:
The compensation of its cheer
Is reason why the grass survives
Of verdurous Christianity,
Ay, trampled, lives, tho' hardly thrives
In these mad days."—
Surprised at it,
Derwent intently viewed the man,
Marked the unsolaced aspect wan;
And fidgeted; yet matter fit
Had offered; but the other changed
In quick caprice, and willful ranged
In wild invective: "O abyss!
Here, upon what was erst the sod,
A man betrayed the yearning god;
A man, yet with a woman's kiss.

'Twas human, that unanimous cry,
'We're fixed to hate him—crucify!'
The which they did. And hands, nailed down,
Might not avail to screen the face
From each head-wagging mocking one.
This day, with some of earthly race,
May passion similar go on?"—
Inferring, rightly or amiss,
Some personal peculiar cause
For such a poignant strain as this,
The priest disturbed not here the pause
Which sudden fell. The other turned,
And, with a strange transition, burned
Invokingly: "Ye trunks of moan—
Gethsemane olives, do ye hear
The trump of that vain-glorious land
Where human nature they enthrone
Displacing the divine?" His hand
He raised there—let it fall, and fell
Himself, with the last syllable,
To moody hush. Then, fierce: "Hired band
Of laureates of man's fallen tribe
Slaves are ye, slaves beyond the scribe
Of Nero; he, if flatterer blind,
Toadied not total human kind,

Which ye kerns do. But Bel shall bow
And Nebo stoop."
"Ah, come, friend, come,
Pleaded the charitable priest
Still bearing with him, anyhow,
By fate unbidden to joy's feast:
"Thou'rt strong; yield then the weak some roon
Too earnest art thou;" and with eye
Of one who fain would mollify
All frowardness, he looked a smile.
But not that heart might he beguile:
Man's vicious: snaffle him with kings;
Or, if kings cease to curb, devise
Severer bit. This garden brings
Such lesson. Heed it, and be wise
In thoughts not new."
"Thou'rt ill to-day,"
Here peering, but in cautious way,
"Nor solace find in valley wild."
The other wheeled, nor more would say;
And soon the cavalcade defiled.

Canto IV - Of Mortmain

"Our friend there—he's a little queer,"
To Rolfe said Derwent riding on;
"Beshrew me, there is in his tone
Naught of your new world's chanticleer.
Who's the eccentric? can you say?"
"Partly; but 'tis at second hand.
At the Black Jew's I met with one
Who, in response to my demand,
Did in a strange disclosure run
Respecting him."—"Repeat it, pray."—
And Rolfe complied. But here receive
Less the details of narrative
Than what the drift and import may convey.

A Swede he was—illicit son
Of noble lady, after-wed,
Who, for a cause over which be thrown
Charity of oblivion dead,—
Bore little love, but rather hate,
Even practiced to ensnare his state.
His father, while not owning, yet
In part discharged the natural debt

Of duty; gave him liberal lore
And timely income; but no more.
Thus isolated, what to bind
But the vague bond of human kind?
The north he left, to Paris came—
Paris, the nurse of many a flame
Evil and good. This son of earth,
This Psalmanazer, made a hearth
In warm desires and schemes for man:
Even he was an Arcadian.
Peace and good will was his acclaim—
If not in words, yet in the aim:
Peace, peace on earth: that note he thrilled,
But scarce in way the cherubs trilled
To Bethlehem and the shepherd band.
Yet much his theory could tell;
And he expounded it so well,
Disciples came. He took his stand.
Europe was in a decade dim:
Upon the future's trembling rim
The comet hovered. His a league
Of frank debate and close intrigue:
Plot, proselyte, appeal, denounce
Conspirator, pamphleteer, at once,
And prophet. Wear and tear and jar
He met with coffee and cigar:
These kept awake the man and mood
And dream. That uncreated Good
He sought, whose absence is the cause
Of creeds and Atheists, mobs and laws.
Precocities of heart outran
The immaturities of brain.
Along with each superior mind
The vain, foolhardy, worthless, blind,
With Judases, are nothing loath
To clasp pledged hands and take the oath
Of aim, the which, if just, demands
Strong hearts, brows deep, and priestly hands.
Experience with her sharper touch
Stung Mortmain: Why, if men prove such,
Dote I? love theory overmuch?
Yea, also, whither will advance
This Revolution sprung in France
So many years ago? where end?

That current takes me. Whither tend?
Come, thou who makest such hot haste
To forge the future—weigh the past.

Such frame he knew. And timed event
Cogent a further question lent:
Wouldst meddle with the state? Well, mount
Thy guns; how many men dost count?
Besides, there's more that here belongs:
Be many questionable wrongs:
By yet more questionable war,
Prophet of peace, these wouldst thou bar?
The world's not new, nor new thy plea.
Tho' even shouldst thou triumph, see,
Prose overtakes the victor's songs:
Victorious right may need redress:
No failure like a harsh success.
Yea, ponder well the historic page:
Of all who, fired with noble rage,
Have warred for right without reprieve,
How many spanned the wings immense
Of Satan's muster, or could cheat
His cunning tactics of retreat
And ambuscade? Oh, now dispense!
The world is portioned out, believe:
The good have but a patch at best,
The wise their corner; for the rest—
Malice divides with ignorance.
And what is stable? find one boon
That is not lackey to the moon
Of fate. The flood ebbs out—the ebb
Floods back; the incessant shuttle shifts
And flies, and weaves and tears the web.
Turn, turn thee to the proof that sifts:
What if the kings in Forty-eight
Fled like the gods? even as the gods
Shall do, return they made; and sate
And fortified their strong abodes;
And, to confirm them there in state,
Contrived new slogans, apt to please—
Pan and the tribal unities.
Behind all this still works some power
Unknowable, thou'lt yet adore.
That steers the world, not man. States drive;
The crazy rafts with billows strive.—
Go, go—absolve thee. Join that band
That wash them with the desert sand
For lack of water. In the dust
Of wisdom sit thee down, and rust.

So mused hc solitary pined.
Tho' his apostolate had thrown

New prospects ope to Adam's kind,
And fame had trumped him far and free—
Now drop he did—a clod unknown;
Nay, rather, he would not disown
Oblivion's volunteer to be;
Like those new-world discoverers bold
Ending in stony convent cold,
Or dying hermits; as if they,
Chastised to Micah's mind austere,
Remorseful felt that ampler sway
Their lead had given for old career
Of human nature.
But this man
No cloister sought. He, under ban
Of strange repentance and last dearth,
Roved the gray places of the earth.
And what seemed most his heart to wring
Was some unrenderable thing:
'Twas not his bastardy, nor bale
Medean in his mother pale,
Nor thwarted aims of high design;
But deeper—deep as nature's mine.
Tho' frequent among kind he sate
Tranquil enough to hold debate,
His moods he had, mad fitful ones
Prolonged or brief, outbursts or moans
And at such times would hiss or cry:
"Fair Circe—goddess of the sty!"
More frequent this: "Mock worse than wrong:
The Syren's kiss—the Fury's thong!"

Such he. Tho' scarce as such portrayed
In full by Rolfe, yet Derwent said
At close: "There's none so far astray,
Detached, abandoned, as might seem,
As to exclude the hope, the dream
Of fair redemption. One fine day
I saw at sea, by bit of deck—
Weedy—adrift from far away—
The dolphin in his gambol light
Through showery spray, arch into sight:
He flung a rainbow o'er that wreck."

Canto V - Clarel and Glaucon

Now slanting toward the mountain's head

They round its southern shoulder so;
That immemorial path they tread
Whereby to Bethany you go
From Salem over Kedron's bed
And Olivet. Free change was made
Among the riders. Lightly strayed,
With overtures of friendly note,
To Clarel's side the Smyrniote.
Wishful from every one to learn,
As well his giddy talk to turn,
Clarel—in simpleness that comes
To students versed more in their tomes
Than life—of Homer spake, a man
With Smyrna linked, born there, 'twas said.
But no, the light Ionian
Scarce knew that singing beggar dead,
Though wight he'd heard of with the name;

"Homer? yes, I remember me;
Saw note-of-hand once with his name:
A fig for him, fig-dealer he,
The veriest old nobody:"
Then lightly skimming on: "Did you
By Joppa come? I did, and rue
Three dumpish days, like Sundays dull
Such as in London late I knew;
The gardens tho' are bountiful.
But Bethlehem—beyond compare!
Such roguish ladies! Tarried there?
You know it is a Christian town,
Decreed so under Ibrahim's rule
The Turk." E'en thus he rippled on,
Way giving to his spirits free,
Relieved from that disparity
Of years he with the banker felt,
Nor noted Clarel's puzzled look,
Who, novice-like, at first mistook,
Doubting lest satire might be dealt.
Adjusting now the sporting gun
Slung to his back with pouch and all:
"Oh, but to sight a bird, just one,
An eagle say, and see him fall."
And, chatting still, with giddy breath,
Of hunting feats over hill and dale:
"Fine shot was mine by Nazareth;

But birding's best in Tempe's Vale:
From Thessalonica, you know,

'Tis thither that we fowlers stray.
But you don't talk, my friend.—Heigh-ho,
Next month I wed; yes, so they say.
Meantime do sing a song or so
To cheer one. Won't? Must I?—Let's see:
Song of poor-devil dandy: he:—
"She's handsome as a jeweled priest
In ephod on the festa.
And each poor blade like me must needs
Idolize and detest her.
"With rain-beads on her odorous hair
From gardens after showers,
All bloom and dew she trips along,
Intent on selling flowers.
"She beams—the rainbow of the bridge;
But, ah, my blank abhorrence,
She buttonholes me with a rose,
This flower-girl of Florence.

"My friends stand by; and, 'There!' she says—
An angel arch, a sinner:
I grudge to pay, but pay I must,
Then—dine on half a dinner!—
"Heigh-ho, next month I marry: well!"
With that he turned aside, and went
Humming another air content.
And Derwent heard him as befell.
"This lad is like a land of springs,"
He said, "he gushes so with song."—
"Nor heeds if Olivet it wrong,"
Said Rolfe; "but no—he sings—he rings;
His is the guinea, fiddle-strings
Of youth too—which may heaven make strong!"
Meanwhile, in tetchy tone austere
That reprobated song and all,
Lowering rode the presbyter,
A cloud whose rain ere long must fall.

Canto VI - The Hamlet

In silence now they pensive win
A slope of upland over hill
Eastward, where heaven and earth be twin
In quiet, and earth seems heaven's sill.
About a hamlet there full low,
Nor cedar, palm, nor olive show—

Three trees by ancient legend claimed
As those whereof the cross was framed.
Nor dairy white, nor well-curb green,
Nor cheerful husbandry was seen,
Though flinty tillage might be named:
Nor less if all showed strange and lone
The peace of God seemed settled down:
Mary and Martha's mountain-town.
To Rolfe the priest said, breathing low:
"How placid! Carmel's beauty here,
If added, could not more endear."—
Rolfe spake not, but he bent his brow.
Aside glanced Clarel on the face
Of meekness; and he mused: In thee
Methinks similitude I trace
To Nature's look in Bethany.
But, ah, and can one dream the dream
That hither thro' the shepherds' gate,
Even by the road we traveled late,
Came Jesus from Jerusalem,
Who pleased him so in fields and bowers,
Yes, crowned with thorns, still loved the flowers?
Poor gardeners here that turned the sod
Friends were they to the Son of God?
And shared He e'en their humble lot?

The sisters here in pastoral plot
Green to the door—did they yield rest,
And bathe the feet, and spread the board
For Him, their own and brother's guest,
The kindly Christ, even man's fraternal Lord?
But see: how with a wandering hand,

In absent-mindedness afloat,
And dreaming of his fairy-land,
Nehemiah smooths the ass's coat.

Canto VII - Guide and Guard

Descending by the mountain side
When crags give way to pastures wide,
And lower opening, ever new,
Glades, meadows, hamlets meet the view
Which from above did coyly hide—
And with re-kindled breasts of spring
The robins thro' the orchard wing;

Excellent then—as there bestowed—
And true in charm the downward road.
Quite other spells an influence throw
Down going, down, to Jericho.
Here first on path so evil-starred
Their guide they scan, and prize the guard.

The guide, a Druze of Lebanon,
Was rumored for an Emir's son,
Or offspring of a lord undone
In Ibrahim's time. Abrupt reverse
The princes in the East may know:
Lawgivers are outlaws at a blow,
And Crœsus dwindles in the purse.
Exiled, cut off, in friendless state,
The Druze maintained an air sedate;
Without the sacrifice of pride,
Sagacious still he earned his bread,
E'en managed to maintain the head,
Yes, lead men still, if but as guide
To pilgrims.
Here his dress to mark:
A simple woolen cloak, with dark
Vertical stripes; a vest to suit;
White turban like snow-wreath: a boot

Exempt from spur; a sash of fair
White linen, long-fringed at the ends:
The garb of Lebanon. His mare
In keeping showed: the saddle plain:
Head-stall untasseled, slender rein.
But nature made her rich amends
For art's default: full eye of flame
Tempered in softness, which became
Womanly sometimes, in desire
To be caressed; ears fine to know
Least intimation, catch a hint
As tinder takes the spark from flint
And steel. Veil-like her clear attire
Of silvery hair, with speckled show
Of grayish spots, and ample flow
Of milky mane. Much like a child
The Druze she'd follow, more than mild.
Not less, at need, what power she'd don,
Clothed with the thunderbolt would run
As concious of the Emir's son
She bore; nor knew the hireling's lash,
Red rowel, or rebuke as rash.

Courteous her treatment. But deem not
This tokened a luxurious lot:
Her diet spare; sole stable, earth;
Beneath the burning sun she'd lie
With mane disheveled, whence her eye
Would flash across the fiery dearth,
As watching for that other queen,
Her mate, a beauteous Palmyrene,
The pride of Tadmore's tented scene.
Athwart the pommel-cloth coarse-spun
A long pipe lay, and longer gun,
With serviceable yataghan.
But prized above these arms of yore,
A new revolver bright he bore
Tucked in the belt, and oft would scan.
Accoutered thus, thro' desert-blight
Whose lord is the Amalekite,
And proffering or peace or war,
The swart Druze rode his silvery Zar.

Behind him, jogging two and two,
Came troopers six of tawny hue,
Bewrinkled veterans, and grave
As Carmel's prophets of the cave:
Old Arab Bethlehemites, with guns
And spears of grandsires old. Weird ones,
Their robes like palls funereal hung
Down from the shoulder, one fold flung
In mufflement about the head,
And kept there by a fillet's braid.

Over this venerable troop
Went Belex doughty in command,
Erst of the Sultan's saucy troop
Which into death he did disband—
Politic Mahmoud—when that clan
By fair pretence, in festive way,
He trapped within the Artmedan—
Of old, Byzantium's circus gay.
But Belex a sultana saved—
His senior, though by love enslaved,
Who fed upon the stripling's May—
Long since, for now his beard was gray;
Tho' goodly yet the features fine,
Firm chin, true lip, nose aquiline—
Type of the pure Osmanli breed.
But ah, equipments gone to seed—
Ah, shabby fate! his vesture's cloth

Hinted the Jew bazaar and moth:
The saddle, too, a cast-off one,
An Aga's erst, and late was sown
With seed-pearl in the seat; but now
All that, with tag-work, all was gone—
The tag-work of wee bells in row
That made a small, snug, dulcet din
About the housings Damascene.

But mark the bay: his twenty years
Still showed him pawing with his peers.
Pure desert air, doled diet pure,
Sleek tendance, brave result insure.
Ample his chest; small head, large eye—
How interrogative with soul—
Responsive too, his master by:
Trim hoof, and pace in strong control.
Thy birth-day well they keep, thou Don,
And well thy birth-day ode they sing;
Nor ill they named thee Solomon,
Prolific sire. Long live the king.

Canto VIII - Rolfe and Derwent

They journey. And, as heretofore,
Derwent invoked his spirits bright
Against the wilds expanding more:
"Do but regard yon Islamite
And horse: equipments be but lean,
Nor less the nature still is rife
Mettle, you see, mettle and mien.
Methinks fair lesson here we glean:
The inherent vigor of man's life
Transmitted from strong Adam down,
Takes no infirmity that's won
By institutions—which, indeed,
Be as equipments of the breed.
God bless the marrow in the bone!
What's Islam now? does Turkey thrive?
Yet Islamite and Turk they wive
And flourish, and the world goes on.
"Ay. But all qualities of race
Which make renown—these yet may die
While leaving unimpaired in grace
The virile power," was Rolfe's reply;
"For witness here I cite a Greek—

God bless him! who tricked me of late
In Argos. What a perfect beak
In contour,—oh, 'twas delicate;
And hero-symmetry of limb:
Clownish I looked by side of him.
Oh, but it does one's ardor damp—
That splendid instrument, a scamp!
These Greeks indeed they wear the kilt
Bravely; they skim their lucid seas;
But, prithee, where is Pericles?
Plato is where? Simonides?
No, friend: much good wine has been spilt:
The rank world prospers; but, alack!
Eden nor Athens shall come back:—
And what's become of Arcady?"
He paused; then in another key:
"Prone, prone are era, man and nation
To slide into a degradation?
With some, to age is that—but that."

"Pathetic grow'st thou," Derwent said:
And lightly, as in leafy glade,
Lightly he in the saddle sat.

Canto IX - Through Adommin

In order meet they take their way
Through Bahurim where David fled;
And Shimei like a beast of prey
Prowled on the side-cliff overhead,
And flung the stone, the stone and curse,
And called it just, the king's reverse:
Still grieving grief, as demons may.

In flanking parched ravine they won,
The student wondered at the bale
So arid, as of Acheron
Run dry. Alert showed Belex hale,
Uprising in the stirrup, clear
Of saddle, outlook so to gain,
Rattling his piece and scimeter.
"Dear me, I say," appealing ran
From the sleek Thessalonian.
"Say on!" the Turk, with bearded grin;
"This is the glen named Adommin!"
Uneasy glance the banker threw,

Tho' first now of such name he knew
Or place. Nor was his flutter stayed
When Belex, heading his brigade,
Drew sword, and with a summons cried:
"Ho, rout them!" and his cohort veered,
Scouring the dens on either side,
Then all together disappeared
Amid wild turns of ugly ground
Which well the sleuth-dog might confound.
The Druze, as if 'twere nothing new—
The Turk doing but as bid to do—
A higher stand-point would command.
But here across his shortened rein
And loosened, shrewd, keen yataghan,
Good Nehemiah laid a hand:
"Djalea, stay—not long I'll be;
A word, one Christian word with ye.
I've just been reading in the place
How, on a time, carles far from grace
Left here half dead the faring man:
Those wicked thieves. But heaven befriends,
Still heaven at need a rescue lends:
Mind ye the Good Samaritan?"—
In patient self-control high-bred,
Half of one sense, an ear, the Druze
Inclined; the while his grave eye fed
Afar; his arms at hand for use.
"He," said the meek one going on,
Naught heeding but the tale he spun,
"He, when he saw him in the snare,
He had compassion; and with care
Him gently wakened from the swound
And oil and wine poured in the wound;
Then set him on his own good beast,
And bare him to the nighest inn—
A man not of his town or kin—
And tended whom he thus released;
Up with him sat he all that night,
Put off he did his journey quite;
And on the morrow, ere he went,
For the mistrustful host he sent,
And taking out his careful purse,
He gave him pence; and thus did sue:
'Beseech ye now that well ye nurse
This poor man whom I leave with you;
And whatsoe'er thou spendest more,
When I again come, I'll restore.'—
Ye mind the chapter? Well, this day

Were some forlorn one here to bleed,
Aid would be meted to his need
By good soul traveling this way.
Speak I amiss? an answer, pray?"—
In deference the armed man,
O'er pistols, gun, and yataghan,
The turban bowed, but nothing said;
Then turned—resumed his purpose. Led
By old traditionary sense,
A liberal, fair reverence,
The Orientals homage pay,
And license yield in tacit way
To men demented, or so deemed.

Derwent meanwhile in saddle there
Heard all, but scarce at ease he seemed,
So ill the tale and time did pair.
Vine whispered to the saint aside:
"There was a Levite and a priest."
"Whom God forgive," he mild replied,
"As I forget;" and there he ceased.
Touching that trouble in advance,
Some here. much like to landsmen wise
At sea in hour which tackle tries,
The adventure's issue left to chance.
In spent return the escort wind
Reporting they had put to flight
Some prowlers.—"Look!" one cried. Behind
A lesser ridge just glide from sight—
Though neither man nor horse appears—
Steel points and hair-tufts of five spears.
Like dorsal fins of sharks they show
When upright these divide the wave
And peer above, while down in grave
Of waters, slide the body lean
And charnel mouth.
With thoughtful mien
The student fared, nor might withstand
The something dubious in the Holy Land.

Canto X - A Halt

In divers ways which vary it
Stones mention find in hallowed Writ:
Stones rolled from well-mouths, altar stones,
Idols of stone, memorial ones,

Sling-stones, stone tables; Bethel high
Saw Jacob, under starry sky,

On stones his head lay—desert bones;
Stones sealed the sepulchers—huge cones
Heaved there in bulk; death too by stones
The law decreed for crime; in spite
As well, for taunt, or type of ban,
The same at place were cast, or man;
Or piled upon the pits of fight
Reproached or even denounced the slain:
So in the wood of Ephraim, some
Laid the great heap over Absalom.
Convenient too at willful need,
Stones prompted many a ruffian deed
And ending oft in parting groans;
By stones died Naboth; stoned to death
Was Stephen meek: and Scripture saith,
Against even Christ they took up stones.
Moreover, as a thing profuse,
Suggestive still in every use,
On stones, still stones, the gospels dwell
In lesson meet or happier parable.

Attesting here the Holy Writ—
In brook, in glen, by tomb and town
In natural way avouching it—
Behold the stones! And never one
A lichen greens; and, turn them o'er—
No worm—no life; but, all the more,
Good witnesses.
The way now led
Where shoals of flints and stones lay dead.
The obstructed horses tripped and stumbled,
The Thessalonian groaned and grumbled.
But Glaucon cried: "Alack the stones!
Or be they pilgrims' broken bones
Wherewith they pave the turnpikes here?
Is this your sort of world, Mynheer?

"Not on your knee no no, no no;
But sit you so: verily and verily
Paris, are you true or no?
I'll look down your eyes and see.

"Helen, look—and look and look;
Look me, Helen, through and through;
Make me out the only rake:

Set down one and carry two."—
"Have done, sir," roared the Elder out;
"Have done with this lewd balladry."—
Amazed the singer turned about;
But when he saw that, past all doubt,
The Scot was in dead earnest. he.
"Oh now, monsieur—monsieur, monsieur!"
Appealing there so winningly—
Conceding, as it were, his age,
Station, and moral gravity,
And right to be morose indeed,
Nor less endeavoring to assuage
At least. But scarce did he succeed.

Rolfe likewise, if in other style,
Here sought that hard road to beguile;
"The stone was man's first missile; yes,
Cain hurled it, or his sullen hand
Therewith made heavy. Cain, confess,
A savage was, although he planned
His altar. Altars such as Cain's
Still find we on far island-chains
Deep mid the woods and hollows dark,
And set offlike the shittim Ark.
Refrain from trespass; with black frown
Each votary straight takes up his stone—
As once against even me indeed:
I see them now start from their rocks
In malediction."
"Yet concede,
They were but touchy in their creed,"
Said Derwent; "but did you succumb?
These irritable orthodox!"—
Thereat the Elder waxed more glum.

A halt being called now with design
Biscuit to bite and sip the wine,
The student saw the turbaned Druze
A courtesy peculiar use
In act of his accosting Vine,
Tho' but in trifle as to how
The saddle suited. And before,
In little things, he'd marked the show
Of like observance. How explore
The cause of this, and understand?

The pilgrims were an equal band:
Why this preferring way toward one?

But Rolfe explained in undertone:
"But few, believe, have nicer eye
For the cast of aristocracy
Than Orientals. Well now, own,
Despite at times a manner shy,
Shows not our countryman in mold
Of a romanced nobility?
His chary speech, his rich still air
Confirm them in conjecture there.
I make slim doubt these people hold
Vine for some lord who fain would go
For delicate cause, incognito.—
What means Sir Crab?"—
In smouldering ire
The Elder, not dismounting, views
The nearer prospect; ill content,
The distance next his glance pursues,
A land of Eblis burned with fire;
Recoils; then, with big eyebrows bent,
Lowers on the comrades—Derwent most,
With luncheon now and flask engrossed;
His bridle turns, adjusts his seat
And holsters where the pistols be,
Nor taking leave like Christian sweet,
(Quite mindless of Paul's courtesy)
With dumb indomitable chin
Straight back he aims thro' Adommin,
Alone, nor blandly self-sustained—
Robber and robber-glen disdained.
As stiff he went, his humor dark
From Vine provoked a vivid spark—
Derisive comment, part restrained.
He passes. Well, peace with him go.
If truth have painted heart but grim,
None here hard measure meant for him;
Nay, Haytian airs around him blow,
And woo and win to cast behind
The harsher and inclement mind.
But needs narrate what followed now.
"Part from us," Derwent cried, "that way?
I fear we have offended. Nay,
What other cause?"—
"The desert, see:
He and the desert don't agree,"
Said Rolfe; "or rather, let me say
He can't provoke a quarrel here
With blank indifference so drear:
Ever the desert waives dispute,

Cares not to argue, bides but mute.
Besides, no topographic cheer:
Surveyor's tape don't come in play;
The same with which upon a day
He upon all fours soused did roam
Measuring the sub-ducts of Siloam.
Late asking him in casual way
Something about the Tomb's old fane,
These words I got: 'Sir, I don't know;
But once I dropped in—not again;
'Tis monkish, 'tis a raree-show—
A raree-show. Saints, sites, and stuff.
Had I my will I'd strip it, strip!'
I knew 'twere vain to try rebuff;
But asked, 'Did Paul, embarked in ship
With Castor and Pollux for a sign
Deem it incumbent there to rip
From stern and prow the name and shrine?'
'Saint Paul, sir, had not zeal enough;
I always thought so;' and went on:
'Where stands this fane, this Calvary one
Alleged? why, sir, within the site
Of Herod's wall? Can that be right?'
But why detail. Suffice, in few,
Even Zion's hill, he doubts that too;
Nay, Sinai in his dry purview
He's dubious if, as placed, it meet
Requirements."

"Why then do his feet
Tread Judah? no good end is won;
Said Derwent.
"Curs need have a bone
To mumble, though but dry nor sweet.
Nay, that's too harsh and overdone.
'Tis still a vice these carpers brew—
They try us—us set carping too."
"Ah well, quick then in thought we'll shun him,
And so foreclose all strictures on him.
Howbeit, this confess off-hand:
Amiss is robed in gown and band
A disenchanter.—Friend, the wine!"
The banker passed it without word.
Sad looked he: Why, these fools are stirred
About a nothing!—Plain to see
Such comradeship did ill agree:
Pedants, and poor! nor used to dine
In ease of table-talk benign—

Steeds, pictures, ladies, gold, Tokay,
Gardens and baths, the English news,
Stamboul, the market—gain or lose?
He turned to where young Glaucon lay,
Who now to startled speech was won:
"Look, is he crazy? see him there!"
The saint it was with busy care
Flinging aside stone after stone,
Yet feebly, nathless as he wrought
In charge imposed though not unloved;
While every stone that he removed
Laid bare but more. The student sighed,
So well he kenned his ways distraught
At influx of his eldritch tide.
But Derwent, hastening to the spot,
Exclaimed, "How now? surely, 'tis not
To mend the way?"
With patient look,
Poising a stone as 'twere a clod:
"All things are possible with God;
The humblest helper will he brook."
Derwent stood dumb; but quick in heart
Conjecturing how it was, addressed
Some friendly words, and slid apart;
And, yet while by that scene impressed,
Came, as it chanced, where unbecalmed
Mortmain aloof sat all disarmed—
Legs lengthwise crossed, head hanging low,
The skull-cap pulled upon the brow,
Hands groping toward the knees: "Then where?
A Thug, the sword-fish roams the sea—
The falcon's pirate in the air;
Betwixt the twain, where shalt thou flee,
Poor flying-fish? whither repair?
What other element for thee?
Whales, mighty whales have felt the wound—
Plunged bleeding thro' the blue profound;
But where their fangs the sand-sharks keep
Be shallows worse than any deep."—
Hardly that chimed with Derwent's bell:
Him too he left.
When it befell
That new they started on their way;
To turn the current or allay,
He talked with Clarel, and first knew
Nehemiah's conceit about the Jew:

The ways prepared, the tilth restored

For the second coming of Our Lord.
Rolfe overheard: "And shall we say
That this is craze? or but, in brief,
Simplicity of plain belief?
The early Christians, how did they?
For His return looked any day."

From dwelling on Rolfe's thought, ere long
On Rolfe himself the student broods:
Surely I would not think a wrong;
Nor less I've shrunk from him in moods.
A bluntness is about him set:

Truth's is it? But he winneth yet
Through taking qualities which join.
Make these the character? the rest
But rim? On Syracusan coin
The barbarous letters shall invest
The relievo's infinite of charm.—
I know not. Does he help, or harm?

Canto XI - Of Deserts

Tho' frequent in the Arabian waste
The pilgrim, up ere dawn of day,
Inhale thy wafted musk, Cathay;
And Adam's primal joy may taste,
Beholding all the pomp of night
Bee'd thick with stars in swarms how bright;
And so, rides on alert and braced—
Tho' brisk at morn the pilgrim start,
Ere long he'll know in weary hour
Small love of deserts, if their power
Make to retreat upon the heart
Their own forsakenness.
Darwin quotes
From Shelley, that forever floats
Over all desert places known,
Mysterious doubt—an awful one.
He quotes, adopts it. Is it true?
Let instinct vouch; let poetry
Science and instinct here agree,
For truth requires strong retinue.

Waste places are where yet is given
A charm, a beauty from the heaven

Above them, and clear air divine—
Translucent a-ther opaline;
And some in evening's early dew
Put on illusion of a guise
Which Tantalus might tantalize
Afresh; ironical unrolled
Like Western counties all in grain
Ripe for the sickleman and wain;
Or, tawnier than the Guinea gold,
More like a lion's skin unfold:
Attest the desert opening out
Direct from Cairo by the Gate
Of Victors, whence the annual rout
To Mecca bound, precipitate
Their turbaned frenzy.—
Sands immense
Impart the oceanic sense:
The flying grit like scud is made:
Pillars of sand which whirl about
Or are along in colonnade,
True kin be to the water-spout.
Yonder on the horizon, red
With storm, see there the caravan
Straggling long-drawn, dispirited;
Mark how it labors like a fleet
Dismasted, which the cross-winds fan
In crippled disaster of retreat
From battle.—
Sinai had renown
Ere thence was rolled the thundered Law;
Ever a terror wrapped its crown;
Never did shepherd dare to draw
Too nigh (Josephus saith) for awe
Of one, some ghost or god austere—
Hermit unknown, dread mountaineer.—
When comes the sun up over Nile
In cloudlessness, what cloud is cast
O'er Lybia? Thou shadow vast
Of Cheops' indissoluble pile,
Typ'st thou the imperishable Past
In empire posthumous and reaching sway
Projected far across to time's remotest day?
But curb.—Such deserts in air-zone
Or object lend suggestive tone,
Redeeming them.
For Judah here—
Let Erebus her rival own:
'Tis horror absolute severe,

Dead, livid, honey-combed, dumb, fell—
A caked depopulated hell;
Yet so created, judged by sense,
And visaged in significance
Of settled anger terrible.
Profoundly cloven through the scene
Winds Kedron—word (the scholar saith)
Importing anguish hard on death.
And aptly may such named ravine
Conduct unto Lot's mortal Sea
In cleavage from Gethsemane
Where it begins.
But why does man
Regard religiously this tract
Cadaverous and under ban
Of blastment? Nay, recall the fact
That in the pagan era old
When bolts, deemed Jove's, tore up the mound,
Great stones the simple peasant rolled
And built a wall about the gap
Deemed hallowed by the thunder-clap.
So here: men here adore this ground
Which doom hath smitten. 'Tis a land
Direful yet holy—blest tho' banned.

But to pure hearts it yields no fear;
And John, he found wild honey here.

Canto XII - The Banker

Infer the wilds which next pertain.
Though travel here be still a walk,
Small heart was theirs for easy talk.

Oblivious of the bridle-rein
Rolfe fell to Lethe altogether,
Bewitched by that uncanny weather
Of sultry cloud. And home-sick grew
The banker. In his reverie blue
The cigarette, a summer friend,
Went out between his teeth—could lend
No solace, soothe him nor engage.
And now disrelished he each word
Of sprightly, harmless persiflage
Wherewith young Glaucon here would fain
Evince a jaunty disregard.

But hush betimes o'ertook the twain—
The more impressive, it may be,
For that the senior, somewhat spent,
Florid overmuch and corpulent,
Labored in lungs, and audibly.
Rolfe, noting that the sufferer's steed
Was far less easy than his own,
Relieved him in his hour of need
By changing with him; then in tone
Aside, half musing, as alone,
"Unwise he is to venture here,
Poor fellow; 'tis but sorry cheer
For Mammon. Ill would it accord
If nabob with asthmatic breath
Lighted on Holbein's Dance of Death
Sly slipped among his prints from Claude.
Cosmetic-users scarce are bold
To face a skull. That sachem old
Whose wigwam is man's heart within—
How taciturn, and yet can speak,
Imparting more than books can win;
Not Pleasure's darling cares to seek
Such counselor: the worse he fares;
Since—heedless, taken unawares—
Arrest he finds.—Look: at yon ground
How starts he now! So Abel's hound
Snuffing his prostrate master wan,
Shrank back from earth's first murdered man.—
But friend, how thrivest?" turning there
To Derwent. He, with altered air,
Made vague rejoinder, nor serene:
His soul, if not cast down, was vexed
By Nature in this dubious scene:
His theory she harsh perplexed—
The more so for wild Mortmain's mien:
And Nehemiah in eldritch cheer:
"Lord, now Thou goest forth from Seir;
Lord, now from Edom marchest Thou!"—

Shunning the Swede—disturbed to know
The saint in strange clairvoyance so,
Clarel yet turned to meet the grace
Of one who not infected dwelt—
Yes, Vine, who shared his horse's pace
In level sameness, as both felt
At home in dearth.
But unconcern
That never knew Vine's thoughtful turn

The venerable escort showed:
True natives of the waste abode,
They moved like insects of the leaf—
Tint, tone adapted to the fief.

Canto XIII - Flight of the Greeks

"King, who betwixt the cross and sword
On ashes died in cowl and cord—
In desert died; and, if thy heart
Betrayed thee not, from life didst part
A martyr for thy martyred Lord;
Anointed one and undefiled—
O warrior manful, tho' a child
In simple faith—St. Louis! rise,
And teach us out of holy eyes
Whence came thy trust."

So Rolfe, and shrank,
Awed by that region dread and great;
Thence led to take to heart the fate
Of one who tried in such a blank,
Believed—and died.
Lurching was seen
An Arab tall, on camel lean,
Up laboring from a glen's remove,
His long lance upright fixed above
The gun across the knee in guard.
So rocks in hollow trough of sea
A wreck with one gaunt mast, and yard
Displaced and slanting toward the lee.
Closer he drew; with visage mute,
Austere in passing made salute.
Such courtesy may vikings lend
Who through the dreary Hecla wend.
Under gun, lance, and scabbard hacked
Pressed Nehemiah; with ado
High he reached up an Arab tract
From the low ass—"Christ's gift to you!"
With clatter of the steel he bore
The lofty nomad bent him o'er
In grave regard. The camel too
Her crane-like neck swerved round to view;
Nor more to camel than to man
Inscrutable the ciphers ran.
But wonted unto arid cheer,

The beast, misjudging, snapped it up
And would have munched, but let it drop;
Her master, poling down his spear
Transfixed the page and brought it near,
Nor stayed his travel.
On they went
Through solitudes, till made intent

By small sharp shots which stirred rebound
In echo. Over upland drear
On tract of less obstructed ground
Came fairly into open sight
A mounted train in tulip plight:
Ten Turks, whereof advanced rode four,
With leveled pistols, left and right
Graceful diverging, as in plume
Feather from feather. So brave room
They make for turning toward each shore
Ambiguous in nooks of blight,
Discharging shots; then reunite,
And, with obeisance bland, adore
Their prince, a fair youth, who, behind—
'Tween favorites of equal age,
Brilliant in paynim equipage
With Eastern dignity how sweet,
Nods to their homage, pleased to mind
Their gallant curvets. Still they meet,
Salute and wheel, and him precede,
As in a pleasure-park or mead.

The escorts join; and some would take
To parley, as is wont. The Druze,
Howbeit, hardly seems to choose
The first advances here to make;
Nor does he shun. Alert is seen
One in voluminous turban green,
Beneath which in that barren place
Sheltered he looks as by the grace
Of shady palm-tuft. Vernal he
In sacerdotal chivalry:
That turban by its hue declares
That the great Prophet's blood he shares:
Kept as the desert stallions be,
'Tis an attested pedigree.
But ah, the bigot, he could lower
In mosque on the intrusive Giaour.
To make him truculent for creed
Family-pride joined personal greed.

Tho' foremost here his word he vents—
Officious in the conference,
In rank and sway he ranged, in sooth,
Behind that fine sultanic youth
Which held his place apart, and, cool,
In lapse or latency of rule
Seemed mindless of the halting train
And pilgrims there of Franquestan
Or land of Franks. Remiss he wore
An indolent look superior.
His grade might justify the air:
The viceroy of Damascus' heir.
His father's jurisdiction sweeps
From Lebanon to Ammon's steeps.
Return he makes from mission far
To independent tribes of war
Beyond the Hauran. In advance
Of the main escort, gun and lance,
He aims for Salem back.
This learned,
In anxiousness the banker yearned
To join; nor Glaucon seemed averse.
'Twas quick resolved, and soon arranged
Through fair diplomacy of purse
And Eastern compliments exchanged.

Their wine, in pannier of the mule,
Upon the pilgrims they bestow:
"And pledge us, friends, in valley cool,
If such this doleful road may know:
Farewell!" And so the Moslem train
Received these Christians, happy twain.

They fled. And thou? The way is dun;
Why further follow the Emir's son?
Scarce yet the thought may well engage
To lure thee thro' these leafless bowers
That little avails a pilgrimage
Whose road but winds among the flowers.
Part here, then, would ye win release
From ampler dearth; part, and in peace.

Nay, part like Glaucon, part with song:
The note receding dies along:
"Tarry never there
Where the air
Lends a lone Hadean spell—

Where the ruin and the wreck
Vine and ivy never deck,
And wizard wan and sibyl dwell:
There, oh, beware!

"Rather seek the grove—
Thither rove,
Where the leaf that falls to ground
In a violet upsprings,
And the oracle that sings
Is the bird above the mound:
There, tarry there!"

Canto XIV - By Anchor

Jerusalem, the mountain town
Is based how far above the sea;
But down, a lead-line's long reach down,
A deep-sea lead, beneath the zone
Of ocean's level, heaven's decree
Has sunk the pool whose deeps submerged
The doomed Pentapolis fire-scourged.
Long then the slope, though varied oft,
From Zion to the seats abject;
For rods and roods ye wind aloft
By verges where the pulse is checked;
And chief both hight and steepness show
Ere Achor's gorge the barrier rends
And like a thunder-cloud impends
Ominous over Jericho.

Hard by the brink the Druze leads on,
But halts at a projecting crown

Of cliff, and beckons them. Nor goat
Nor fowler ranging far and high
Scales such a steep; nor vulture's eye
Scans one more lone. Deep down in throat
It shows a sooty black.
"A forge
Abandoned," Rolfe said, "thus may look."
"Yea," quoth the saint, "and read the Book:
Flames, flames have forked in Achor's gorge.
His wizard vehemence surprised:
Some new illusion they surmised;
Not less authentic text he took:

"Yea, after slaughter made at Ai
When Joshua's three thousand fled,
Achan the thief they made to die—
They stoned him in this hollow here
They burned him with his children dear;
Among them flung his ingot red
And scarlet robe of Babylon:
Meet end for Carmi's wicked son
Because of whom they failed at Ai:
'Twas meet the trespasser should die;
Yea, verily."—His visage took
The tone of that uncanny nook.
To Rolfe here Derwent: "Study him;
Then weigh that most ungenial rule
Of Moses and the austere school
Which e'en our saint can make so grim—
At least while Achor feeds his eyes."
"But here speaks Nature otherwise?"
Asked Rolfe; "in region roundabout
She's Calvinistic if devout
In all her aspect."—
Vine, o'ercast,
Estranged rode in thought's hid repast.
Clarel, receptive, saw and heard,
Learning, unlearning, word by word.
Erelong the wilds condense the ill—
They hump it into that black Hill
Named from the Forty Days and Nights,
The Quarantania's sum of blights.
Up from the gorge it grows, it grows:
Hight sheer, sheer depth, and death's repose.
Sunk in the gulf the wave disowns,
Stranded lay ancient torrent-stones.
These Mortmain marks: "Ah, from your deep
Turn ye, appeal ye to the steep?
But that looks off, and everywhere
Descries but worlds more waste, more bare."

Flanked by the crag and glen they go.
Ahead, erelong in greeting show
The mounts of Moab, o'er the vale
Of Jordan opening into view,
With cloud-born shadows sweeping thro'.
The Swede, intent: "Lo, how they trail,
The mortcloths in the funeral
Of gods!"
Although he naught confessed,
In Derwent, marking there the scene,

What interference was expressed
As of harsh grit in oiled machine—
Disrelish grating interest:
Howbeit, this he tried to screen.
"Pisgah!" cried Rolfe, and pointed him.
"Peor, too—ay, long Abarim
The ridge. Well, well: for thee I sigh,
Poor Moses. Saving Jericho
And her famed palms in Memphian row,
No cheerful landscape met thine eye;
Unless indeed (yon Pisgah's high)
Was caught, beyond each mount and plain,
The blue, blue Mediterranean."
"And might he then for Egypt sigh?"
Here prompted Rolfe; but no reply;
And Rolfe went on: "Balboa's ken
Roved in fine sweep from Darien:
The woods and waves in tropic meeting,
Bright capes advancing, bays retreating—
Green land, blue sea in charm competing!"

Meantime, with slant reverted eyes
Vine marked the Crag of Agonies.
Exceeding high (as Matthew saith)
It shows from skirt of that wild path
Bare as an iceberg seamed by rain
Toppling awash in foggy main
Off Labrador. Grottoes Vine viewed
Upon the flank—or cells or tombs—
Void as the iceberg's catacombs
Of frost. He starts. A form endued
With living guise, from ledges dim
Leans as if looking down toward him.
Not pointing out the thing he saw
Vine watched it, but it showed no claw
Of hostile purpose; tho' indeed
Robbers and outlaws armed have dwelt
Vigilant by those caves where knelt
Of old the hermits of the creed

Beyond, they win a storied fount
Which underneath the higher mount
Gurgles, clay-white, and downward sets
Toward Jericho in rivulets,
Which—much like children whose small mirth
Not funerals can stay—through dearth
Run babbling. One old humpbacked tree,
Sad grandam whom no season charms

Droops o'er the spring her withered arms;
And stones as in a ruin laid,
Like penitential benches be
Where silent thickets fling a shade
And gather dust. Here halting, here
while they rest and try the cheer.

Canto XV - The Fountain

It brake, it brake how long ago,
That morn which saw thy marvel done,
Elisha—healing of the spring!
A good deed lives, the doer low:
See how the waters eager run
With bounty which they chiming bring:
So out of Eden's bounds afar
Hymned Pison through green Havilah!
But ill those words in tone impart
The simple feelings in the heart
Of Nehemiah—full of the theme,
Standing beside the marge, with cup,
And pearls of water-beads adroop
Down thinnish beard of silvery gleam.
"Truly," said Derwent, glad to note
That Achor found her antidote,
"Truly, the fount wells grateful here."
Then to the student: "For the rest,
The site is pleasant; nor unblest
These thickets by their shade endear."
Assent half vacant Clarel gave,
Watching that miracle the wave.
Said Rolfe, reclining by the rill,
"Needs life must end or soon or late:
Perchance set down it is in fate
That fail I must ere we fulfill
Our travel. Should it happen true—
Attention, pray—I mend my will,
And name executors in you:
Bury me by the road, somewhere
Near spring or brook. Palms plant me there,
And seats with backs to them, all stone:
In peace then go. The years shall run,
And green my grave shall be, and play
The part of host to all that stray
In desert: water, shade, and rest
Their entertainment. So I'll win

Balm to my soul by each poor guest
That solaced leaves the Dead Man's Inn.
But charges, mind, yourselves defray—
Seeing I've naught."
Where thrown he lay,
Vine, sensitive, suffused did show,
Yet looked not up, but seemed to weigh
The nature of the heart whose trim
Of quaint good fellowship could so
Strike on a chord long slack in him.
But how may spirit quick and deep
A constancy unfreakish keep?
A reed there shaken fitfully
He marks: "Was't this we came to see
In wilderness?" and rueful smiled.
The meek one, otherwise beguiled,
Here chancing now the ass to note
Languidly munching straw and bran,
Drew nigh, and smoothed the roughened coat,
And gave her bread, the wheaten grain.
Vine watches; and his aspect knows
A flush of diffident humor: "Nay,
Me too, me too let wait, I pray,
On our snubbed kin here;" and he rose.

Erelong, alert the escort show:
'Tis stirrups. But the Swede moved not,
Aloof abiding in dark plot
Made by the deeper shadow: "Go—
My horse lead; but for me, I stay
Some bread—there, that small loaf will do:
It is my whim—my whim, I say;
Mount, heed not me."—"And how long, pray?
Asked Derwent, startled: "eve draws on:
Ye would not tarry here alone?"
"Thou man of God, nor desert here,
Nor Zin, nor Obi, yieldeth fear
If God but be- but be! This waste—
Soon shall night fold the hemisphere;
But safer then to lay me down,
Here, by yon evil Summit faced—
Safer than in the cut-throat town
Though on the church-steps. Go from me—
Begone! To-morrow or next day
Jordan ye greet, then round ye sway
And win Lot's marge. In sight ye'll be:
I'll intercept. Ride on, go—nay,
Bewitched, why gape ye so at me?

Shall man not take the natural way
With nature? Tut, fling me the cloak!"
Away, precipitate he broke,
The skull-cap glooming thro' the glade:
They paused, nor ventured to invade.

While so, not unconcerned, they stood,
The Druze said, "Well, let be. Why chafe?
Nights here are mild; one's pretty safe
When fearless.—Belex! come, the road!"

Canto XVI - Night in Jericho

Look how a pine in luckless land
By fires autumnal overrun,
Abides a black extinguished brand
Gigantic—killed, not overthrown;
And high upon the horny bough
Perches the bandit captain-crow
And caws unto his troop afar
Of foragers: much so, in scar
Of blastment, looms the Crusaders' Tower
On the waste verge of Jericho:
So the dun sheik in lawless power
Kings it aloft in sombre robe,
Lord of the tawny Arab mob
To which, upon the plains in view,
He shouts down his wild hullabaloo.

There on the tower, through eve's delay
The pilgrims tarry, till for boon,
Launched up from Nebo far away,
Balloon-like rose the nibbled moon—
Nibbled, being after full one day.
Intent they watched the planet's rise—
Familiar, tho' in strangest skies.
The ascending orb of furrowed gold,
Contracting, changed, and silvery rolled
In violet heaven. The desert brown,
Dipped in the dream of argent light,
Like iron plated, took a tone
Transmuting it; and Ammon shone
In peaks of Paradise—so bright.
They gazed. Rolfe brake upon the calm:
"O haunted place, O powerful charm!
Were now Elijah's chariot seen

(And yonder, read we writ aright,
He went up—over against this site)
Soaring in that deep heaven serene,
To me 'twould but in beauty rise;
Nor hair-clad John would now surprise
But Volney!"
"Volney?" Derwent cried;
"Ah, yes; he came to Jordan's side
A pilgrim deist from the Seine."
"Ay, and Chateaubriand, he too,
The Catholic pilgrim, hither drew—

Here formed his purpose to assert
Religion in her just desert
Against the Red Caps of his time.
The book he wrote; it dies away;
But those Septemberists of crime
Enlarge in Vitriolists to-day.
Nor while we dwell upon this scene
Can one forget poor Lamartine
A latter palmer. Oh, believe
When, his fine social dream to grieve,
Strode Fate, that realist how grim,
Displacing, deriding, hushing him,
Apt comment then might memory weave
In lesson from this waste.—That cry!
And would the jackal testify
From Moab?"
Derwent could but sway:
"Omit ye in citation, pray,
The healthy pilgrims of times old?
Robust they were; and cheery saw
Shrines, chapels, castles without flaw
Now gone. That river convent's fold,
By willows nigh the Pilgrims' Strand
Of Jordan, was a famous hold.
Prince Sigurd from the Norseman land,
Quitting his keel at Joppa, crossed
Hither, with Baldwin for his host,
And Templars for a guard. Perchance
Under these walls the train might prance
By Norman warder eyed."
"Maybe,"
Responded Vine; "but why disown
The Knight of the Leopard—even he,
Since hereabout that fount made moan,
Named Diamond of the Desert?"—"Yes,"
Beamed Rolfe, divining him in clue;

"Such shadows we, one need confess
That Scott's dreamed knight seems all but true
As men which history vouches. She—
Tasso's Armida, by Lot's sea,
Where that enchantress, with sweet look
Of kindliest human sympathy,
Such webs about Rinaldo wove
That all the hero he forsook—
Lost in the perfidies of love—
Armida—starts at fancy's bid
Not less than Rahab, lass which hid
The spies here in this Jericho. "

A lull. Their thoughts, mute plunging, strayed
Like Arethusa under ground;
While Clarel marked where slumber-bound
Lay Nehemiah in screening shade.

Erelong, in reappearing tide,
Rolfe, gazing forth on either side:
"How lifeless! But the annual rout
At Easter here, shall throng and shout,
Far populate the lonely plain,
(Next day a solitude again,)
All pressing unto Jordan's dew;
While in the saddle of disdain
Skirr the Turk guards with fierce halloo,
Armed herdsmen of the drove." He ceased;
And fell the silence unreleased
Till yet again did Rolfe round peer
Upon that moonlit land of fear:
"Man sprang from deserts: at the touch
Of grief or trial overmuch,
On deserts he falls back at need;
Yes, 'tis the bare abandoned home
Recalleth then. See how the Swede
Like any rustic crazy Tom,
Bursting through every code and ward
Of civilization, masque and fraud,
Takes the wild plunge. Who so secure,
Except his clay be sodden loam,
As never to dream the day may come
When he may take it, foul or pure?
What in these turns of mortal tides—
What any fellow-creature bides,
May hap to any."
"Pardon, pray,"
Cried Derwent—"but 'twill quick away:

Yon moon in pearl-cloud: look, her face
Peers like a bride's from webs of lace."
They gazed until it faded there:
When Rolfe with a discouraged air
Sat as rebuked. In winning strain,
As 'twere in penitence urbane,
Here Derwent, "Come, we wait thee now."
"No matter," Rolfe said; "let it go.
My earnestness myself decry;
But as heaven made me, so am I."

"You spake of Mortmain," breathed Vine low.
As embers, not yet cold, will catch
Quick at the touch of smallest match,
Here Rolfe: "In gusts of lonely pain
Beating upon the naked brain—"
"God help him, ay, poor realist!"
So Derwent. and that theme dismissed

When Ashtoreth her zenith won,
Sleep drugged them and the winds made moan.

Canto XVII - In Mid-Watch

Disturbed by topics canvassed late,
Clarel, from dreams of like debate,
Started, and heard strange muffled sounds,
Outgivings of wild mountain bounds.
He rose, stood gazing toward the hight—
Bethinking him that there away
Behind it o'er the desert lay
The walls that sheltered Ruth that night—
When Rolfe drew near. With motion slight,
Scarce conscious of the thing he did,
Partly aside the student slid;
Then, quick as thought, would fain atone.
Whence came that shrinking start unbid?
But from desire to be alone?
Or skim or sound him, was Rolfe one
Whom honest heart would care to shun?
By spirit immature or dim
Was nothing to be learned from him?
How frank seemed Rolfe. Yet Vine could lure
Despite reserve which overture
Withstood—e'en Clarel's—late repealed,
Finding that heart a fountain sealed.

But Rolfe: however it might be—
Whether in friendly fair advance
Checked by that start of dissonance,
Or whether rapt in revery
Beyond—apart he moved, and leant
Down peering from the battlement
Upon its shadow. Then and there
Clarel first noted in his air
A gleam of oneness more than Vine's—
The irrelation of a weed
Detached from vast Sargasso's mead
And drifting where the clear sea shines.
But Clarel turned him; and anew
His thoughts regained their prior clew;
When, lo, a fog, and all was changed.
Crept vapors from the Sea of Salt,
Overspread the plain, nor there made halt,
But blurred the heaven.
            As one estranged
Who watches, watches from the shore,
Till the white speck is seen no more,
The ship that bears his plighted maid,
Then turns and sighs as fears invade;
See here the student, repossessed
By thoughts of Ruth, with eyes late pressed
Whither lay Salem, close and wynd—
The mist before him, mist behind,
While intercepting memories ran
Of chant and bier Armenian.

Canto XVIII - The Syrian Monk

At early hour with Rolfe and Vine
Clarel ascends a minor hight;
They overtake in lone recline
A strange wayfarer of the night
Who, 'twixt the small hour and the gray,
With cruze and scrip replenished late
In Jericho at the wattled gate,
Had started on the upland way:
A young strange man of aspect thin
From vigils which in fast begin.
Though, pinned together with the thorn,
His robe was ragged all and worn—
Pure did he show as mountain-leaf

By brook, or coral washed in reef.
Contrasting with the bleached head-dress
His skin revealed such swarthiness,
And in the contour clear and grace
So all unworldly was the face,
He looked a later Baptist John.
They start; surprise perforce they own:
Much like De Gama's men, may be,
When sudden on their prow at sea
Lit the strange bird from shores unknown.
Although at first from words he shrunk,
He was, they knew, a Syrian monk.
They so prevailed with him and pressed,
He longer lingered at request.
They won him over in the end
To tell his story and unbend.

He told how that for forty days,
Not yet elapsed, he dwelt in ways
Of yonder Quarantanian hight,
A true recluse, an anchorite;
And only came at whiles below,
And ever in the calm of night,
To beg for scraps in Jericho.
'Twas sin, he said, that drove him out
Into the desert—sin of doubt.
Even he it was upon the mount
By chance perceived, untold, by Vine,
From Achor's brink. He gave account
Of much besides; his lonely mine
Of deep illusion; how the night,
The first, was spent upon the hight,
And way he climbed:
"Up cliff, up crag—
Cleft crag and cliff which still retard,
Goat-like I scrambled where stones lag
Poised on the brinks by thunder marred.
A ledge I reached which midway hung
Where a hut-oratory clung—
Rude stones massed up, with cave-like door,
Eremite work of days of yore.
White bones here lay, remains of feast
Dragged in by bird of prey or beast.
Hence gazed I on the wilds beneath,
Dengadda and the coasts of death.
But not a tremor felt I here:
It was upon the summit fear
First fell; there first I saw this world;

And scarce man's place it seemed to be;
The mazed Gehennas so were curled
As worm-tracks under bark of tree.
I ween not if to ye 'tis known—
Since few do know the crag aright,
Years left unvisited and lone—
That a wrecked chapel marks the site
Where tempter and the tempted stood
Of old. I sat me down to brood
Within that ruin; and—my heart
Unwaveringly to set apart
In meditation upon Him
Who here endured the evil whim
Of Satan—steadfast, steadfast down
Mine eyes fixed on a flinty stone
Which lay there at my feet. But thought
Would wander. Then the stone I caught,
Convulsed it in my hand till blood
Oozed from these nails. Then came and stood
The Saviour there—the Imp and He:
Fair showed the Fiend—foul enemy;
But, ah, the Other pale and dim:
I saw but as the shade of Him.

That passed. Again I was alone—
Alone—ah, no—not long alone:
As glides into dead grass the snake
Lean rustling from the bedded brake,
A spirit entered me. 'Twas he,
The tempter, in return; but me
He tempted now. He mocked: 'Why strife?
Dost hunger for the bread of life?
Thou lackest faith: faith would be fed;
True faith could turn that stone to bread,
That stone thou hold'st.'—Mute then my face
I lifted to the starry space;
But the great heaven it burned so bright,
It cowed me, and back fell my sight.
Then he: 'Is yon the Father's home?
And thou His child cast out to night?
'Tis bravely lighted, yonder dome.'—
'Part speak'st thou true: yea, He is there.'—
'Yea, yea, and He is everywhere—
Now and for aye, Evil and He.'—
'Is there no good?'—'Ill to fulfill
Needful is good: good salts the ill.'—
'He's just.'—'Goodness is justice. See,
Through all the pirate-spider's snare

Of silken arcs of gossamer,
'Tis delicate geometry:
Adorest the artificer?'—
No answer knew I, save this way:
'Faith bideth.'—'Noon, and wait for day?
The sand's half run! Eternal, He:
But aye with a futurity
Which not exceeds his past. Agree,
Full time has lapsed. What ages hoar,
What period fix, when faith no more,
If unfulfilled, shall fool?'—I sat;
Sore quivered I to answer that,
Yet answered naught; but lowly said—
'And death?'—'Why beat the bush in thee?
It is the cunningest mystery:

Alive thou know'st not death; and, dead,
Death thou'lt not know.'—'The grave will test;
But He, He is, though doubt attend;
Peace will He give ere come the end.'—
'Ha, thou at peace? Nay, peace were best—
Could the unselfish yearner rest!
At peace to be, here, here on earth,
Where peace, heart-peace, how few may claim,
And each pure nature pines in dearth—
Fie, fie, thy soul might well take shame.'—
There sunk my heart—he spake so true
In that. O God (I prayed), come through
The cloud; hard task Thou settest man
To know Thee; take me back again
To nothing, or make clear my view!—
Then stole the whisper intermitting;
Like tenon into mortice fitting
It slipped into the frame of me:
'Content thee: in conclusion caught
Thou'lt find how thought's extremes agree,—
The forethought clinched by afterthought,
The firstling by finality.'—
There close fell, and therewith the stone
Dropped from my hand.—His will be done!"
And skyward patient he appealed,
Raising his eyes, and so revealed
First to the pilgrims' waiting view
Their virginal violet of hue.

Rolfe spake: "Surely, not all we've heard:
Peace—solace—was in end conferred?"—
His head but fell. He rose in haste,

The rough hair-girdle tighter drew
About the hollow of the waist,
Departing with a mild adieu.

They sat in silence. Rolfe at last:
"And this but ecstasy of fast?
Construe then Tonah in despair."—
The student turned, awaiting Vine;
Who answered nothing, plaiting there
A weed from neighboring ground uptorn,
Plant common enough in Palestine,
And by the peasants named Christ's Thorn.

Canto XIX - An Apostate

"Barque, Easter barque, with happier freight
Than Leon's spoil of Inca plate;
Which vernal glidest from the strand
Of statues poised like angels fair;
On March morn sailest—starting, fanned
Auspicious by Sardinian air;
And carriest boughs thro' Calpe's gate
To Norman ports and Belgian land,
That the Green Sunday, even there,
No substituted leaf may wear,
Holly or willow's lither wand,
But sprays of Christ's canonic tree,
Rome's Palma-Christi by decree,
The Date Palm; ah, in bounty launch,
Thou blessed Easter barque, to me
Hither one consecrated branch!"

So Rolfe in burst, and turned toward Vine;
But he the thorn-wreath still did twine.
Rolfe watched him busy there and dumb,
Then cried: "Did gardens favor it,
How would I match thee here, and sit
Wreathing Christ's flower, chrysanthemum."

Erelong the Syrian they view
In slow ascent, and also two
Between him and the peak,—one wight
An Arab with a pouch, nor light,
A desert Friday to the one
Who went before him, coming down,
Shagged Crusoe, by the mountain spur.

This last, when he the votary meets
Sad climbing slow, him loudly greets,
Stopping with questions which refer
In some way to the crag amort—
The crag, since thitherward his hand
Frequent he waves, as with demand
For some exact and clear report
Touching the place of his retreat
Aloft. As seemed, in neutral plight
Submiss responds the anchorite,
The wallet dropped beside his feet.
These part. Master and man now ply
Yet down the slope; and he in van—
Round-shouldered, and tho' gray yet spry—
A hammer swung.
                  I've met that man
Elsewhere (thought Clarel)—he whose cry
And gibe came up from the dung-gate
In hollow, when we scarce did wait
His nearer speech and wagging head,
The saint and I.—But naught he said
Hereof.
        The stranger closer drew;
And Rolfe breathed "This now is a Jew,—
German, I deem—but readvised—
An Israelite, say, Hegelized—
Convert to science, for but see
The hammer: yes, geology."
                            As now the other's random sight
On Clarel mute and Vine is thrown,
He misinterprets their grave plight;
And, with a banter in the tone,
Amused he cries: "Now, now, yon hight—
Come, let it not alarm: a mount
Whereof I've taken strict account
(Its first geologist, believe),
And, if my eyes do not deceive,
'Tis Jura limestone, every spur;
Yes, and tho' signs the rocks imprint
Which of Plutonic action hint,
No track is found, I plump aver,
Of Pluto's footings—Lucifer."

The punning mock and manner stirred
Repugnance in fastidious Vine;
But Rolfe, who tolerantly heard,
Parleyed, and won him to define
At large his rovings on the hight.

The yester-afternoon and night
He'd spent there, sleeping in a cave—
Part for adventure, part to spite
The superstition, and outbrave.
'Twas a severe ascent, he said;
In bits a ladder of steep stone
With toe-holes cut, and worn, each one
By eremites long centuries dead.
And of his cullings too he told:
His henchman here, the Arab wight,
Bare solid texts from Bible old—
True Rock of Ages, he averred.
To read before a learned board,
When home regained should meet his sight,
A monograph he would indite
The theme, that crag.
He went his way,
To win the tower. Little they say;
But Clarel started at the view
Which showed opposed the anchorite
Ascetical and—such a Jew.

Canto XX - Under the Mountain

From Ur of the Chaldees roved the man—
Priest, shepherd, prince, and pioneer—
Swart Bedouin in time's dusky van;
Even he which first, with mind austere,
Arrived in solitary tone
To think of God as One—alone;
The first which brake with hearth and home
For conscience' sake; whom piety ruled,
Prosperity blest, longevity schooled,
And time in fullness brought to Mamre's tomb
Arch founder of the solid base of Christendom.
Even this. For why disown the debt
When vouchers be? Yet, yet and yet
Our saving salt of grace is due
All to the East—nor least the Jew.
Perverse, if stigma then survive,
Elsewhere let such in satire thrive—
Not here. Quite other end is won
In picturing Margoth, fallen son
Of Judah. Him may Gabriel mend.

Little for love, or to unbend,
But swayed by tidings, hard to sift,

Of robbers by the river-drift
In force recruited; they suspend
Their going hence to Jordan's trees.
Released from travel, in good hour
Nehemiah dozed within the tower.
Uplands they range, and woo the breeze
Where crumbled aqueducts and mounds
Override long slopes and terraces,
And shattered pottery abounds—
Or such would seem, yet may but be
The shards of tile-like brick dispersed
Binding the wall or bulwark erst,
Such as in Kent still serve that end
In Richborough castle by the sea—
A Roman hold. What breadth of doom
As of the worlds in strata penned—
So cosmic seems the wreck of Rome.
Not wholly proof to natural sway
Of serious hearts and manners mild,
Uncouthly Margoth shared the way.
He controverted all the wild,
And in especial, Sodom's strand
Of marl and clinker: "Sirs, heed me:
This total tract," and Esau's hand
He waved; "the plain—the vale—Lot's sea—
It needs we scientists remand
Back from old theologic myth
To geologic hammers. Pray,
Let me but give ye here the pith:
As the Phlegraean fields no more
Befool men as the spookish shore
Where Jove felled giants, but are known—
The Solfatara and each cone
Volcanic—to be but on a par
With all things natural; even so
Siddim shall likewise be set far
From fable."
                Part overhearing this,
Derwent, in rear with Rolfe: "Old clo'!
We've heard all that, and long ago:
Conceit of vacant emphasis:
Well, well!"—Here archly, Rolfe: "But own,
How graceful your concession—won
A score or two of years gone by.
Nor less therefrom at need ye'll fly,
Allow. Scarce easy 'tis to hit
Each slippery turn of cleric wit."
Derwent but laughed; then said—"But he:

Intelligence veneers his mien
Though rude: unprofitably keen:
Sterile, and with sterility
Self-satisfied." "But this is odd!
Not often do we hear you rail:
The gown it seems does yet avail,
Since from the sleeve you draw the rod.
But look, they lounge."
Yes, all recline,
And on the site where havoc clove
The last late palm of royal line,
Sad Montezuma of the grove.

The mountain of the Imp they see
Scowl at the freedom which they take
Relaxed beneath his very lee.
The bread of wisdom here to break,
Margoth holds forth: the gossip tells
Of things the prophets left unsaid—
With master-key unlocks the spells
And mysteries of the world unmade;
Then mentions Salem: "Stale is she!
Lay flat the walls, let in the air,
That folk no more may sicken there!
Wake up the dead; and let there be
Rails, wires, from Olivet to the sea,
With station in Gethsemane."
The priest here flushed. Rolfe rose: and, "How—
You go too far!" "A long Dutch mile
Behind the genius of our time."
"Explain that, pray." "And don't you know?
Mambrino's helmet is sublime—
The barber's basin may be vile:
Whether this basin is that helm
To vast debate has given rise—
Question profound for blinking eyes;
But common sense throughout her realm
Has settled it."

There, like vain wight
His fine thing said, bidding friends good night,
He, to explore a rift they see,
Parted, bequeathing, as might be,
A glance which said—Again ye'll pine
Left to yourselves here in decline,
Missing my brave vitality!

Derwent fetched breath: "A healthy man:
His lungs are of the soundest leather."
"Health's insolence in a Saurian,"
Said Rolfe. With that they fell together
Probing the purport of the Jew
In last ambiguous words he threw.
But Derwent, and in lenient way,
Explained it.
    "Let him have his say,"
Cried Rolfe; "for one I spare defiance
With such a kangaroo of science."
"Yes; qualify though," Derwent said,
"For science has her eagles too."
Here musefully Rolfe hung the head;
Then lifted: "Eagles? ay; but few.
And search we in their a-ries lone
What find we, pray? perchance, a bone."
"A very cheerful point of view!"
"'Tis as one takes it. Not unknown
That even in Physics much late lore
But drudges after Plato's theme;
Or supplements—but little more—
Some Hindoo's speculative dream
Of thousand years ago. And, own,
Darwin is but his grandsire's son."
"But Newton and his gravitation!"
"Think you that system's strong persuasion
Is founded beyond shock? O'ermuch
'Twould seem for man, a clod, to clutch
God's secret so, and on a slate
Cipher all out, and formulate
The universe." "You Pyrrhonist!
Why, now, perhaps you do not see—
Your mind has taken such a twist—
The claims of stellar chemistry."
"What's that?" "No matter. Time runs on
And much that's useful, grant, is won."
"Yes; but more's claimed. Now first they tell
The human mind is free to range.
Enlargement—ay; but where's the change?
We're yet within the citadel—
May rove in bounds, and study out
The insuperable towers about."

"Come; but there's many a merry man:

How long since these sad times began?"
That steadied Rolfe: "Where's no annoy
I too perchance can take a joy—
Yet scarce in solitude of thought:
Together cymbals need be brought
Ere mirth is made. The wight alone
Who laughs, is deemed a witless one.
And why? But that we'll leave unsought."
"By all means!—O ye frolic shapes:
Thou Dancing Faun, thou Faun with Grapes!
What think ye of them? tell us, pray.
"Fine mellow marbles."
"But their hint?"
"A mine as deep as rich the mint
Of cordial joy in Nature's sway
Shared somewhere by anterior clay
When life was innocent and free:
Methinks 'tis this they hint to me."
He paused, as one who makes review
Of gala days; then—warmly too—
"Whither hast fled, thou deity
So genial? In thy last and best,
Best avatar—so ripe in form—
Pure as the sleet—as roses warm—
Our earth's unmerited fair guest—
A god with peasants went abreast:
Man clasped a deity's offered hand;
And woman, ministrant, was then
How true, even in a Magdalen.
Him following through the wilding flowers
By lake and hill, or glad detained
In Cana—ever out of doors—
Ere yet the disenchantment gained
What dream they knew, that primal band
Of gipsy Christians! But it died;
Back rolled the world's effacing tide:
The 'world'—by Him denounced, defined—
Him first—set off and countersigned,
Once and for all, as opposite
To honest children of the light.
But worse cam— creeds, wars, stakes. Oh, men
Made earth inhuman; yes, a den
Worse for Christ's coming, since his love
(Perverted) did but venom prove.
In part that's passed. But what remains
After fierce seethings? golden grains?
Nay, dubious dregs: be frank, and own.
Opinion eats; all crumbles down:

Where stretched an isthmus, rolls a strait:
Cut off, cut off! Can'st feel elate
While all the depths of Being moan,
Though luminous on every hand,
The breadths of shallow knowledge more expand?
Much as a light-ship keeper pines
Mid shoals immense, where dreary shines
His lamp, we toss beneath the ray
Of Science' beacon. This to trim
Is now man's barren office.—Nay,"
Starting abrupt, "this earnest way
I hate. Let doubt alone; best skim,
Not dive."
"No, no," cried Derwent gay,
Who late, upon acquaintance more,
Took no mislike to Rolfe at core,
And fain would make his knell a chime—
Being pledged to hold the palmy time
Of hope at least, not to admit
That serious check might come to it:
"No, sun doubt's root—'twill fade, 'twill fade!
And for thy picture of the Prime,
Green Christianity in glade—
Why, let it pass; 'tis good, in sooth:
Who summons poets to the truth?"
How Vine sidelong regarded him
As 'twere in envy of his gift
For light disposings: so to skim!

Clarel surmised the expression's drift,
Thereby anew was led to sift
Good Derwent's mind. For Rolfe's discourse
Prior recoil from Margoth's jeer
Was less than startled shying here
At earnest comment's random force.
He shrunk; but owned 'twas weakness mere.
Himself he chid: No more for me
The petty half-antipathy:
This pressure it need be endured:
Weakness to strength must get inured;
And Rolfe is sterling, though not less
At variance with that parlor-strain
Which counts each thought that borders pain
A social treason. Sterling—yes,
Despite illogical wild range
Of brain and heart's impulsive counterchange.

As by the wood drifts thistle-down
And settles on soft mosses fair,
Stillness was wafted, dropped and sown;
Which stillness Vine, with timorous air
Of virgin tact, thus brake upon,

Nor with chance hint: "One can't forbear
Thinking that Margoth is—a Jew."
Hereat, as for response, they view
The priest.
"And, well, why me?" he cried;
"With one consent why turn to me?
Am I professional? Nay, free!
I grant that here by Judah's side
Queerly it jars with frame implied
To list this geologic Jew
His way Jehovah's world construe:
In Gentile 'twould not seem so odd.
But here may preconceptions thrall?

Be many Hebrews we recall
Whose contrast with the breastplate bright
Of Aaron flushed in altarlight,
And Horeb's Moses, rock and rod,
Or closeted alone with God,
Quite equals Margoth's in its way:
At home we meet them every day.
The Houndsditch clothesman scarce would seem
Akin to seers. For one, I deem
Jew banker, merchant, statesman—these,
With artist, actress known to fame,
All strenuous in each Gentile aim,
Are Nature's off-hand witnesses
There's nothing mystic in her reign:
Your Jew's like wheat from Pharaoh's tomb:
Sow it in England, what will come?
The weird old seed yields market grain."
Pleased by his wit while some recline,
A smile uncertain lighted Vine,
But died away.
"Jews share the change,"
Derwent proceeded: "Range, they range—
In liberal sciences they roam;
They're leavened, and it works, believe;
Signs are, and such as scarce deceive:

From Holland, that historic home
Of erudite Israel, many a tome
Talmudic, shipped is over sea
For antiquarian rubbish."
"Rest!"
Cried Rolfe; "e'en that indeed may be,
Nor less the Jew keep fealty
To ancient rites. Aaron's gemmed vest
Will long outlive Genevan cloth—
Nothing in Time's old camphor-chest
So little subject to the moth.
But Rabbis have their troublers too.
Nay, if thro' dusty stalls we look,
Haply we disinter to view
More than one bold freethinking Jew

That in his day with vigor shook
Faith's leaning tower."
"Which stood the throe,"
Here Derwent in appendix: "look,
Faith's leaning tower was founded so:
Faith leaned from the beginning; yes,
If slant, she holds her steadfastness. "
"May be;" and paused: "but wherefore clog?—
Uriel Acosta, he was one
Who troubled much the synagogue
Recanted then, and dropped undone:
A suicide. There's Heine, too,
(In lineage crossed by blood of Jew,)
Pale jester, to whom life was yet
A tragic farce; whose wild death-rattle,
In which all voids and hollows met,
Desperately maintained the battle
Betwixt the dirge and castanet.
But him leave to his Paris stone
And rail, and friendly wreath thereon.
Recall those Hebrews, which of old
Sharing some doubts we moderns rue,
Would fain Eclectic comfort fold
By grafting slips from Plato's palm
On Moses' melancholy yew:

But did they sprout? So we seek balm
By kindred graftings. Is that true?"
"Why ask? But see: there lived a Jew—
No Alexandrine Greekish one
You know him—Moses Mendelssohn."
"Is't him you cite? True spirit staid,

He, though his honest heart was scourged
By doubt Judaic, never laid
His burden at Christ's door; he urged—
'Admit the mounting flames enfold
My basement; wisely shall my feet
The attic win, for safe retreat?' "
"And he said that? Poor man, he's cold.
But was not this that Mendelssohn
Whose Hebrew kinswoman's Hebrew son,
Baptized to Christian, worthily won
The good name of Neander so?"
"If that link were, well might one urge
From such example, thy strange flow,
Conviction! Breaking habit's tether,
Sincerest minds will yet diverge
Like chance-clouds scattered by mere weather;
Nor less at one point still they meet:
The self-hood keep they pure and sweet."

"But Margoth," in reminder here
Breathed Vine, as if while yet the ray
Lit Rolfe, to try his further cheer:
"But Margoth!"
"He, poor sheep astray,
The Levitie cipher quite erased,
On what vile pig-weed hath he grazed.
Not his Spinosa's starry brow
(A non-conformer, ye'll allow),
A lion in brain, in life a lamb,
Sinless recluse of Amsterdam;
Who, in the obscure and humble lane,
Such strangers seemed to entertain
As sat by tent beneath the tree
On Mamre's plain—mysterious three,
The informing guests of Abraham.
But no, it had but ill beseemed
If God's own angels so could list
To visit one, Pan's Atheist.
That high intelligence but dreamed—
Above delusion's vulgar plain
Deluded still. The erring twain,
Spinosa and poor Margoth here,
Both Jews, which in dissent do vary:
In these what parted poles appear—
The blind man and the visionary."
"And whose the eye that sees aright,
If any?" Clarel eager asked.
Aside Rolfe turned as overtasked;

And none responded. 'Twas like night
Descending from the seats of light,
Or seeming thence to fall. But here
Sedate a kindly tempered look
Private and confidential spoke
From Derwent's eyes, Clarel to cheer:
Take heart; something to fit thy youth
Instill I may, some saving truth—
Not best just now to volunteer.
Thought Clarel: Pray, and what wouldst prove?
Thy faith an over-easy glove.

Meanwhile Vine had relapsed. They saw
In silence the heart's shadow draw—
Rich shadow, such as gardens keep
In bower aside, where glow-worms peep
In evening over the virgin bed
Where dark-green periwinkles sleep—
Their bud the Violet of the Dead.

Canto XXIII - By the Jordan

On the third morn, a misty one,
Equipped they sally for the wave
Of Jordan. With his escort brown

The Israelite attendance gave
For that one day and night alone.
Slung by a cord from saddle-bow,
Is it the mace of Ivanhoe?
Rolfe views, and comments: "Note, I pray,
He said to Derwent on the way,
"Yon knightly hammer. 'Tis with that
He stuns, and would exterminate
Your creeds as dragons."
With light fire
Of wit, the priest rejoinder threw;
But turned to look at Nehemiah:
The laboring ass with much ado

Of swerving neck would, at the sight
Of bramble-tops, snatch for a bite;
And though it bred him joltings ill—
In patience that did never tire,
Her rider let her have her will.
The apostate, ready with his sneer:

"Yes, you had better—'tis a she."
To Rolfe said Derwent: "There, you see:
It is these infidels that jeer
At everything."
                 The Jew withheld
His mare, and let Nehemiah pass:
"Who is this Balaam on the ass?"
But none his wonderment dispelled.

Now skies distill a vaporous rain;
So looked the sunken slimy plain—
Such semblance of the vacuum shared,
As 'twere the quaking sea-bed bared
By the Caracas. All was still:
So much the more their bosoms thrill
With dream of some withdrawn vast surge
Its timed return about to urge
And whelm them.
                 But a cry they hear:
The steed of Mortmain, led in rear,
Broke loose and ran. "Horse too run mad?"
Cried Derwent; "shares his rider's mind—
His rider late? shun both their kind?
Poor Swede! But where was it he said
We should rejoin?" "'Tis by Lot's sea,
Remember. And, pray heaven, it be!—
Look, the steed's caught."
                 Suspicious ground
They skirt, with ugly bushes crowned;
And there into, against surprise,
The vigilant Spahi throws his eyes;
To take of distant chance a bond,
Djalea looks forward, and beyond.

At this, some riders feel that awe
Which comes of sense of absent law,
And irreligious human kind,
Relapsed, remanded, reassigned
To chaos and brute passions blind.
But is it Jordan, Jordan dear,
That doth that evil bound define
Which borders on the barbarous sphere—
Jordan, even Jordan, stream divine?
In Clarel ran such revery here.

Belex his flint adjusts and rights,
Sharp speaks unto his Bethlehemites;
Then, signaled by Djalea, through air

Surveys the further ridges bare.
Foreshortened 'gainst a long-sloped hight
Beyond the wave whose wash of foam
Beats to the base of Moab home,
Seven furious horsemen fling their flight
Like eagles when they launching rush
To snatch the prey that hies to bush.
Dwarfed so these look, while yet afar
Descried. But trusting in their star,
Onward a space the party push;
But halt is called; the Druze rides on,
Bids Belex stand, and goes alone.

Now, for the nonce, those speeders sink
Viewless behind the arborous brink.
Thereto the staid one rides—peers in—
Then waves a hand. They gain his side,
Meeting the river's rapid tide
Here sluicing through embowered ravine
Such as of yore was Midian's screen
For rites impure. Facing, and near,
Across the waves which intervene,
In shade the robbers reappear:
Swart, sinuous men on silvery steeds—
Abreast, save where the copse impedes.
At halt, and mute, and in the van
Confronting them, with lengthy gun
Athwart the knee, and hand thereon,
Djalea waits. The mare and man
Show like a stone equestrian
Set up for homage. Over there
'Twas hard for mounted men to move
Among the thickets interwove,
Which dipped the stream and made a snare.
But, undeterred, the riders press
This way and that among the branches,
Picking them lanes through each recess,
Till backward on their settling haunches
The steeds withstand the slippery slope,
While yet their outflung fore-feet grope;
Then, like sword-push that ends in lunge,
The slide becomes a weltering plunge:
The willows drip, the banks resound;
They halloo, and with spray are crowned.
The torrent, swelled by Lebanon rains,
The spirited horses bravely stem,
Snorting, half-blinded by their manes,
Nor let the current master them.

As the rope-dancer on the hair
Poises the long slim pole in air;
Twirling their slender spears in pride,
Each horseman in imperiled seat
Blends skill and grace with courage meet.
Soon as they win the hither side,
Like quicksilver to beach they glide,
Dismounting, and essay the steep,
The horses led by slackened rein:
Slippery foothold ill they keep.
To help a grim one of the band
Good Nehemiah with mickle strain
Down reaches a decrepit hand:
The sheik ignores it—bandit dun,
Foremost in stride as first in rank—
Rejects it, and the knoll is won.

Challengingly he stares around,
Then stakes his spear upon the bank
As one reclaiming rightful ground.
Like otters when to land they go,
Riders and steeds how sleekly show.
The first inquiring look they trace
Is gun by gun, as face by face:
Salute they yield, for arms they view
Inspire respect sincere and true.
Meantime, while in their bearing shows
The thought which still their life attends,
And habit of encountering foes—
The thought that strangers scarce are friends—
What think the horses? Zar must needs
Be sociable; the robber steeds
She whinnies to; even fain would sway
Neck across neck in lovesome way.
Great Solomon, of rakish strain,
Trumpets—would be Don John again.
The sheik, without a moment's doubt,
Djalea for captain singles out;
And, after parley brief, would fain
Handle that pistol of the guide,
The new revolver at his side.
The Druze assents, nor shows surprise.
Barrel, cap, screw, the Arab tries;
And ah, the contrast needs he own:
Alack, for his poor lance and gun,
Though heirlooms both: the piece in stock
Half honeycombed, with cumbrous lock;
The spear like some crusader's pole

Dropped long ago when death-damps stole
Over the knight in Richard's host,
Then left to warp by Acre lost:
Dry rib of lance. But turning now
Upon his sweetheart, he was cheered:
Her eye he met, the violet-glow,
Peaked ear, the mane's redundant flow;
It heartened him, and round he veered;
Elate he shot a brigand glare:
I, Ishmael, have my desert mare!

Elicited by contact's touch,
Tyrannous spleen vexed Belex much
Mis-liking in poor tribe to mark
Freedom unawed and nature's spark.
With tutoring glance, a tempered fire,
The Druze repressed the illiberal ire.
The silvered saint came gently near
Meekly intrepid, tract in hand,
And reached it with a heart sincere
Unto the sheik, whose fingers spanned
The shrewd revolver, loath to let
That coveted bauble go as yet.
"Nay," breathed the Druze, and gently here:
"The print he likes not; let him be;
Pray now, he deems it sorcery."
They drew him back. In rufflement
The sheik threw round a questioning eye;
Djalea explained, and drew more nigh,
Recalling him to old content;
Regained the weapon; and, from stores
Kept for such need, wary he pours
A dole of powder.
So they part—
Recrossing Jordan, horse and gun,
With warrior cry and brandished dart
Where, in the years whose goal is won
The halcyon Teacher waded in with John.

Canto XXIV - The River-Rite

And do the clear sands pure and cold
At last each virgin elf enfold?
Under what drift of silvery spar
Sleeps now thy servant, Holy Rood,

Which in the age of brotherhood
Approaching here Bethabara
By wilds the verse depicted late,
Of Jordan caught a fortunate
Fair twinkle starry under trees;
And, with his crossed palms heartward pressed,
Bowed him, or dropped on reverent knees,
Warbling that hymn of beauty blest—
The Ave maris stella?—Lo,
The mound of him do field-mice know?
Nor less the rite, a rule serene,
Appropriate in tender grace,
Became the custom of the place
With each devouter Frank.
A truce
Here following the din profuse
Of Moab's swimming robbers keen,
Rolfe, late enamored of the spell
Of rituals olden, thought it well
To observe the Latin usage: "Look,"
Showing a small convenient book
In vellum bound; embossed thereon,
'Tween angels with a rosy crown,
Viols, Cecilia on a throne:
"Thanks, friar Benignus Muscatel;
Thy gift I prize, given me in cell

Of St. John's convent.—Comrades, come!
If heaven delight in spirits glad,
And men were all for brothers made,
Grudge not, beseech, to joy with Rome;"
And launched the hymn. Quick to rejoice,
The liberal priest lent tenor voice;
And marking them in cheery bloom
On turf inviting, even Vine,
Ravished from his reserve supine,
Drew near and overlooked the page—
All self-surprised he overlooked,
Joining his note impulsively;
Yet, flushing, seemed as scarce he brooked

This joy. Was joy a novelty?
Fraternal thus, the group engage—
While now the sun, obscured before,
Illumed for time the wooded shore—
In tribute to the beach and tide.
The triple voices blending glide,
Assimilating more and more,

Till in the last ascriptive line
Which thrones the Father, lauds the Son,
Came concord full, completion fine—
Rapport of souls in harmony of tone.

Meantime Nehemiah, eager bent,
Instinctive caught the sentiment;
But checked himself; and, in mixed mood,
Uncertain or relapsing stood,
Till ere the singers cease to thrill,
His joy is stayed. How cometh this?
True feeling, steadfast faith are his,
While they at best do but fulfill
A transient, an esthetic glow;
Knew he at last—could he but know—
The rite was alien? that no form
Approved was his, which here might warm
Meet channel for emotion's tide?
Apart he went, scarce satisfied;
But presently slipped down to where
The river ran, and tasting spare,
Not quaffing, sighed, "As sugar sweet!"
Though unsweet was it from the flow
Of turbid, troubled waters fleet.
Now Margoth—who had paced the strand
Gauging the level of the land,
Computing part the Jordan's fall
From Merom's spring, and therewithal
Had ended with a river-sip,
Which straight he spewed—here curled the lip
At hearing Nehemiah: The fool!
Fool meek and fulsome like to this—
Too old again to go to school—
Was never! wonder who he is:
I'll ask himself.—"Who art thou, say?"
"The chief of sinners."—"Lack-a-day,
I think so too;" and moved away,
Low muttering in his ill content
At that so Christian bafflement;
And hunted up his sumpter mule
Intent on lunch. A pair hard by
He found. The third some person sly
In deeper shade had hitched—more cool.
This was that mule whose rarer wine,
In pannier slung and blushing shy,
The Thessalonian did decline
Away with him in flight to take,
And friendly gave them when farewell he spake.

Canto XXV - The Dominican

"Ah Rome, your tie! may child clean part?
Nay, tugs the mother at the heart!"

Strange voice that was which three there heard
Reclined upon the bank. They turned;
And he, the speaker of the word,
Stood in the grass, with eyes that burned
How eloquent upon the group.
"Here urging on before our troop,"
He said, "I caught your choral strains—
Spurred quicker, lighted, tied my mule
Behind yon clump; and, for my pains,
Meet—three, I ween, who slight the rule
Of Rome, yet thence do here indeed,
Through strong compulsion of the need,
Derive fair rite: or may I err?"
Surprise they knew, yet made a stir
Of welcome, gazing on the man
In white robe of Dominican,
Of aspect strong, though cheek was spare,
Yellowed with tinge athlete may wear
Whom rigorous masters overtrain
When they with scourge of more and more
Would macerate him into power.
Inwrought herewith was yet the air
And open frontage frankly fair
Of one who'd moved in active scene
And swayed men where they most convene.
His party came from Saba last,
Camping by Lot's wave overnight—
French pilgrims. So he did recite
Being questioned. Thereupon they passed
To matters of more pith. Debate
They held, built on that hymning late;
Till in reply to Derwent's strain
Thus warmed he, that Dominican:
"Crafty is Rome, you deem? Her art
Is simple, quarried from the heart.
Rough marbles, rudiments of worth
Ye win from ledges under earth;
Ye trim them, fit them, make them shine
In structures of a fair design.
Well, fervors as obscure in birth—

Precious, though fleeting in their dates—
Rome culls, adapts, perpetuates
In ordered rites. 'Tis these supply
Means to the mass to beautify
The rude emotion; lend meet voice
To organs which would fain rejoice
But lack the song; and oft present
To sorrow bound, an instrument
Which liberates. Each hope, each fear
Between the christening and the bier
Still Rome provides for, and with grace
And tact which hardly find a place
In uninspired designs."
"Let be
Thou Paul! shall Festus yield to thee?"

Cried Rolfe; "and yet," in altered tone,
"Even these fair things—ah, change goes on!"
"Change? yes, but not with us. In rout
Sword-hilts rap at the Vatican,
And, lo, an old, old man comes out:
'What would ye?' 'Change!' 'I never change.' "
"Things changing not when all things change
Need perish then, one might retort,
Nor err."
"Ay, things of human sort."
"Rome superhuman?"
"As ye will.
Brave schemes these boyish times instill;
But Rome has lived a thousand years:
Shall not a thousand years know more
Than nonage may?" "Then all the cheers
Which hail the good time deemed at door
Are but the brayings which attest
The foolish, many-headed beast!"
"Hardly that inference I own.
The people once elected me
To be their spokesman. In this gown
I sat in legislative hall
A champion of true liberty—
God's liberty for one and all—
Not Satan's license. Mine's the state
Of a staunch Catholic Democrat."
Indulgent here was Derwent's smile,
Incredulous was Rolfe's. But he:
"Hardly those terms ye reconcile.
And yet what is it that we see?
Before the Church our human race

Stand equal. None attain to place
Therein through claim of birth or fee.
No monk so mean but he may dare
Aspire to sit in Peter's chair."
"Why, true," said Derwent; "but what then?
That sums not all. And what think men?"
And, briefly, more, about the rot

Of Rome in Luther's time, the canker spot.
"Well," said the monk, "I'll not gainsay
Some things you put: I own the shame:
Reform was needed, yes, and came—
Reform within. But let that go—
That era's gone: how fares it now?—
Melancthon! was forecast by thee,
Who fain had tempered Luther's mind,
This riot of reason quite set free:
Sects—sects bisected—sects disbanded
Into plain deists underhanded?
Against all this stands Rome's array:
Rome is the Protestant to-day:
The Red Republic slinging flame
In Europe—she's your Scarlet Dame.
Rome stands; but who may tell the end?
Relapse barbaric may impend,
Dismission into ages blind—
Moral dispersion of mankind.
Ah, God," and dropped upon the knee:
"These flocks which range so far from Thee,
Ah, leave them not to be undone:
Let them not cower as 'twixt the sea
And storm—in panic crowd and drown!"
He rose, resumed his previous cheer
With something of a bearing sweet.
"Brother," said Derwent friendly here
"I'm glad to know ye, glad to meet,
Even though, in part, your Rome seeks ends
Not mine. But, see, there pass your friends:
Call they your name?"
                    "Yes, yes" he said,
And rose to loose his mule; "you're right;
We go to win the further bed
Of Jordan, by the convent's site.
A parting word: Methinks ye hold
Reserved objections. I'll unfold
But one:—Rome being fixed in form,
Unyielding there, how may she keep
Adjustment with new times? But deep

Below rigidities of form
The invisible nerves and tissues change
Adaptively. As men that range
From clime to clime, from zone to zone
(Say Russian hosts that menace Ind)
Through all vicissitudes still find
The body acclimate itself
While form and function hold their own—
Again they call:—Well, you are wise;
Enough—you can analogize
And take my meaning: I have done.
No, one more point:—Science but deals
With Nature; Nature is not God;
Never she answers our appeals,
Or, if she do, but mocks the clod.
Call to the echo—it returns
The word you send; how thrive the ferns
About the ruined house of prayer
In woods; one shadow falleth yet
From Christian spire—Turk minaret:
Consider the indifference there.
'Tis so throughout. Shall Science then
Which solely dealeth with this thing
Named Nature, shall she ever bring
One solitary hope to men?

'Tis Abba Father that we seek,
Not the Artificer. I speak,
But scarce may utter. Let it be.
Adieu; remember—Oh, not me;
But if with years should fail delight
As things unmask abroad and home;
Then, should ye yearn in reason's spite,
Remember hospitable Rome."

He turned, and would have gone; but, no,
New matter struck him: "Ere I go
Yet one word more; and bear with me:
Whatever your belief may be—

If well ye wish to human kind,
Be not so mad, unblest, and blind
As, in such days as these, to try
To pull down Rome. If Rome could fall
'Twould not be Rome alone, but all
Religion. All with Rome have tie,
Even the railers which deny,
All but the downright Anarchist,

Christ-hater, Red, and Vitriolist.
Could libertine dreams true hope disable,
Rome's tomb would prove Abaddon's cradle.
Weigh well the Pope. Though he should be
Despoiled of Charlemagne's great fee—
Cast forth, and made a begging friar,
That would not quell him. No, the higher
Rome's In excelsis would extol
Her God—her De profundis roll
The deeper. Let destructives mind
The reserves upon reserves behind.
Offence I mean not. More's to tell:
But frigates meet—hail—part. Farewell."
And, going, he a verse did weave,
Or hummed in low recitative:
"Yearly for a thousand years
On Christmas Day the wreath appears,
And the people joy together:
Prithee, Prince or Parliament,
An equal holiday invent
Outlasting centuries of weather.

"Arrested by a trembling shell,
Wee tinkle of the small mass-bell,
A giant drops upon the knee.
Thou art wise—effect as much;
Let thy wisdom by a touch
Reverence like this decree."

Canto XXVI - Of Rome

"Patcher of the rotten cloth,
Pickler of the wing o' the moth,
Toaster of bread stale in date,
Tinker of the rusty plate,
Botcher of a crumbling tomb,
Pounder with the holy hammer,
Gaffer-gammer, gaffer-gammer—
Rome!
The broker take your trumpery pix,
Paten and chalice! Turn ye—lo,
Here's bread, here's wine. In Mexico
Earthquakes lay flat your crucifix:
All, all's geology, I trow.
Away to your Pope Joan—go!"

As he the robed one decorous went,
From copse that doggerel was sent
And after-cry. Half screened from view
'Twas Margoth, who, reclined at lunch,
Had overheard, nor spared to munch,
And thence his contumely threw.
Rolfe, rising, had replied thereto,
And with some heat, but Derwent's hand
Caught at his skirt: "Nay, of what use?
But wind, foul wind."—Here fell a truce,
Which Margoth could but understand;

Wiping his mouth he hied away.
The student who apart though near
Had heard the Frank with tingling cheer,
Awaited now the after-play
Of comment; and it followed: "Own,"
Said Rolfe, "he took no shallow tone,
That new St. Dominick. Who'll repay?
Wilt thou?" to Derwent turning.—"No,
Not I! But had our Scot been near
To meet your Papal nuncio!
Fight fire with fire. But for me here,

You must have marked I did abstain.—
Odd, odd: this man who'd make our age
To Hildebrand's an appanage—
So able too—lit by our light—
Curious, he should so requite!
And, yes, lurked somewhat in his strain—"
"And in his falling on the knee?"
"Those supple hinges I let be."
"Is the man false?"
"No, hardly that.
'Tis difficult to tell. But see:
Doubt late was an aristocrat;
But now the barbers' clerks do swell
In cast clothes of the infidel;
The more then one can now believe,
The more one's differenced, perceive,
From ribald commonplace. Here Rome
Comes in. This intellectual man—
Half monk, half tribune, partisan—
Who, as he hints—'tis troublesome
To analyze, and thankless too:
Much better be a dove, and coo
Softly. Come then, I'll e'en agree
His manner has a certain lure,

Disinterested, earnest, pure
And liberal. 'Tis such as he
Win over men."
"There's Rome, her camp
Of tried instruction. She can stamp,
On the recruit that's framed aright,
The bearing of a Bayard knight
Ecclesiastic. I applaud
Her swordsmen of the priestly sword
Wielded in spiritual fight."
"Indeed? take care! Rome lacks not charm
For fervid souls. Arm ye, forearm!
For syrens has she too,—her race
Of sainted virgin ones, with grace
Beyond the grace of Grecian calm,

For this is chill, but that how warm."
"A frank concession." "To be sure!
Since Rome may never me allure
By her enticing arts; since all
The bias of the days that be
Away leans from Authority,
And most when hierarchical;
So that the future of the Pope
Is cast in no fair horoscope;
In brief, since Rome must still decay;
Less care I to disown or hide
Aught that she has of merit rare:
Her legends—some are sweet as May;
Ungarnered wealth no doubt is there,
(Too long ignored by Luther's pride)
But which perchance in days divine
(Era, whereof I read the sign)
When much that sours the sects is gone,
Like Dorian myths the bards shall own—
Yes, prove the poet's second mine."
"All that," said Rolfe, "is very fine;
But Rome subsists, she lives to-day,
She re-affirms herself, her sway
Seductive draws rich minds away;
Some pastures, too, yield many a rover:
Sheep, sheep and shepherd running over.

"Such sheep and shepherds, let them go;
They are not legion: and you know
What draws. Little imports it all
Overbalanced by that tidal fall
Of Rome in Southern Europe. Come."

"If the tide fall or here or there,
Be sure 'tis rolling in elsewhere."
"So oceanic then is Rome?"
"Nay, but there's ample sea-verge left:
A hemisphere invites.—When reft
From Afric, and the East its home,
The church shot out through wild and wood—
Germany, Gaul and Britain, Spain—
Colonized, Latinized, and made good
Her loss, and more resolved to reign."
"Centuries, centuries long ago!
What's that to us? I am surprised.
Rome's guns are spiked; and they'll stay so.
The world is now too civilized
For Rome. Your noble Western soil—
What! that be given up for spoil
To—to—"
"There is an Unforeseen.
Fate never gives a guarantee
That she'll abstain from aught. And men
Get tired at last of being free—
Whether in states—in states or creeds.
For what's the sequel? Verily,
Laws scribbled by law-breakers, creeds
Scrawled by the freethinkers, and deeds
Shameful and shameless. Men get sick
Under that curse of Frederick
The cynical: For punishment
This rebel province I present
To the philosophers. But, how?
Whole nations now philosophize,
And do their own undoing now.—
Who's gained by all the sacrifice
Of Europe's revolutions? who?
The Protestant? the Liberal?
I do not think it—not at all:
Rome and the Atheist have gained:
These two shall fight it out—these two;
Protestantism being retained
For base of operations sly
By Atheism."
Without reply
Derwent low whistled—twitched a spray
That overhung: "What tree is this?"
"The tree of knowledge, I dare say;
But you don't eat."—"That's not amiss,"

The good man laughed; but, changing, "O,

That a New-Worlder should talk so!"
"'Tis the New World that mannered me,
Yes, gave me this vile liberty
To reverence naught, not even herself."
"How say you? you're the queerest elf!
But here's a thought I still pursue
A thought I dreamed each thinker knew:
No more can men be what they've been;
All's altered—earth's another scene."
"Man's heart is what it used to be."
"I don't know that."
"But Rome does, though:
And hence her stout persistency.
What mean her re-adopted modes
Even in the enemy's abodes?
Their place old emblems reassume.
She bides—content to let but blow
Among the sects that peak and pine,
Incursions of her taking bloom."
"The censer's musk?—'Tis not the vine,
Vine evangelic, branching out
In fruitful latitude benign,
With all her bounty roundabout—
Each cluster, shaded or in sun,
Still varying from each other one,
But all true members, all with wine
Derived from Christ their stem and stock;
'Tis scarce that vine which doth unlock
The fragrance that you hint of. No,
The Latin plant don't flourish so;
Of sad distemper 'tis the seat;
Pry close, and startled you shall meet
Parasite-bugs—black swarming ones."
"The monks?"—"You jest: thinned out, those drones
Considerate uncommitted eyes
Charged with things manifold and wise,
Rolfe turned upon good Derwent here;
Then changed: "Fall back we must. Yon mule
With pannier: Come, in stream we'll cool
The wine ere quaffing.—Muleteer!"

Canto XXVII - Vine and Clarel

While now, to serve the pilgrim train,
The Arabs willow branches hew,
(For palms they serve in dearth of true),

Or, kneeling by the margin, stoop
To brim memorial bottles up;
And the Greek's wine entices two:
Apart see Clarel here incline,
Perplexed by that Dominican,
Nor less by Rolfe—capricious man:
"I cannot penetrate him.—Vine?"
As were Venetian slats between,
He espied him through a leafy screen,
Luxurious there in umbrage thrown,
Light sprays above his temples blown—
The river through the green retreat
Hurrying, reveling by his feet.
Vine looked an overture, but said
Nothing, till Clarel leaned—half laid—
Beside him: then "We dream, or be
In sylvan John's baptistery:
May Pisa's equal beauty keep?—
But how bad habits persevere!
I have been moralizing here
Like any imbecile: as thus:
Look how these willows over-weep
The waves, and plain: 'Fleet so from us?
And wherefore? whitherward away?
Your best is here where wildings sway
And the light shadow's blown about;
Ah, tarry, for at hand's a sea
Whence ye shall never issue out
Once in.' They sing back: 'So let be!

We mad-caps hymn it as we flow—
Short life and merry! be it so!' "
Surprised at such a fluent turn,
The student did but listen—learn.

Putting aside the twigs which screened,
Again Vine spake, and lightly leaned
"Look; in yon vault so leafy dark,
At deep end lit by gemmy spark
Of mellowed sunbeam in a snare;
Over the stream—ay, just through there—
The sheik on that celestial mare
Shot, fading.—Clan of outcast Hagar,
Well do ye come by spear and dagger!
Yet in your bearing ye outvie
Our western Red Men, chiefs that stalk
In mud paint—whirl the tomahawk.—
But in these Nimrods noted you

The natural language of the eye,
Burning or liquid, flame or dew,
As still the changeable quick mood
Made transit in the wayward blood?
Methought therein one might espy,
For all the wildness, thoughts refined
By the old Asia's dreamful mind;
But hark—a bird?"
Pure as the rain
Which diamondeth with lucid grain,
The white swan in the April hours
Floating between two sunny showers
Upon the lake, while buds unroll;
So pure, so virginal in shrine
Of true unworldliness looked Vine.
Ah, clear sweet ether of the soul
(Mused Clarel), holding him in view.
Prior advances unreturned
Not here he recked of, while he yearned—
O, now but for communion true
And close; let go each alien theme;
Give me thyself!

But Vine, at will
Dwelling upon his wayward dream,
Nor as suspecting Clarel's thrill
Of personal longing, rambled still;
"Methinks they show a lingering trace
Of some quite unrecorded race
Such as the Book of Job implies.
What ages of refinings wise
Must have forerun what there is writ—
More ages than have followed it.
At Lydda late, as chance would have,
Some tribesmen from the south I saw,
Their tents pitched in the Gothic nave,
The ruined one. Disowning law,
Not lawless lived they; no, indeed;
Their chief—why, one of Sydney's clan,
A slayer, but chivalric man;
And chivalry, with all that breed
Was Arabic or Saracen
In source, they tell. But, as men stray
Further from Ararat away
Pity it were did they recede
In carriage, manners, and the rest;
But no, for ours the palm indeed
In bland amenities far West!

Come now, for pastime let's complain;
Grudged thanks, Columbus, for thy main!
Put back, as 'twere—assigned by fate
To fight crude Nature o'er again,
By slow degrees we re-create.
But then, alas, in Arab camps
No lack, they say, no lack of scamps."
Divided mind knew Clarel here;
The heart's desire did interfere.
Thought he, How pleasant in another
Such sallies, or in thee, if said
After confidings that should wed
Our souls in one:—Ah, call me brother!—
So feminine his passionate mood
Which, long as hungering unfed,
All else rejected or withstood.
Some inklings he let fall. But no:
Here over Vine there slid a change
A shadow, such as thin may show
Gliding along the mountain-range
And deepening in the gorge below.
Does Vine's rebukeful dusking say—
Why, on this vernal bank to-day,
Why bring oblations of thy pain
To one who hath his share? here fain
Would lap him in a chance reprieve?
Lives none can help ye; that believe.
Art thou the first soul tried by doubt?
Shalt prove the last? Go, live it out.
But for thy fonder dream of love
In man toward man—the soul's caress—
The negatives of flesh should prove
Analogies of non-cordialness
In spirit.—E'en such conceits could cling
To Clarel's dream of vain surmise
And imputation full of sting.
But, glancing up, unwarned he saw
What serious softness in those eyes
Bent on him. Shyly they withdraw.
Enslaver, wouldst thou but fool me

With bitter-sweet, sly sorcery,
Pride's pastime? or wouldst thou indeed,
Since things unspoken may impede,
Let flow thy nature but for bar?—
Nay, dizzard, sick these feelings are;
How findest place within thy heart
For such solicitudes apart

From Ruth?—Self-taxings.
But a sign
Came here indicative from Vine,
Who with a reverent hushed air
His view directed toward the glade
Beyond, wherein a niche was made
Of leafage, and a kneeler there,
The meek one, on whom, as he prayed,
A golden shaft of mellow light,
Oblique through vernal cleft above,
And making his pale forehead bright,
Scintillant fell. By such a beam
From heaven descended erst the dove
On Christ emerging from the stream.
It faded; 'twas a transient ray;
And, quite unconseious of its sheen,
The suppliant rose and moved away,
Not dreaming that he had been seen.

When next they saw that innocent,
From prayer such cordial had he won
That all his aspect of content
As with the oil of gladness shone.
Less aged looked he. And his cheer
Took language in an action here:
The train now mustering in line,
Each pilgrim with a river-palm
In hand (except indeed the Jew),
The saint the head-stall need entwine
With wreathage of the same. When new
They issued from the wood, no charm
The ass found in such idle gear
Superfluous: with her long ear
She flapped it off, and the next thrust
Of hoof imprinted it in dust.
Meek hands (mused Vine), vainly ye twist
Fair garland for the realist.
The Hebrew, noting whither bent
Vine's glance, a word in passing lent:
"Ho, tell us how it comes to be
That thou who rank'st not with beginners
Regard have for yon chief of sinners."
"Yon chief of sinners?"
"So names he
Himself. For one I'll not express
How I do loathe such lowliness."

Southward they file. 'Tis Pluto's park
Beslimed as after baleful flood:
A nitrous, filmed and pallid mud,
With shrubs to match. Salt specks they mark
Or mildewed stunted twigs unclean
Brushed by the stirrup, Stygean green,
With shrivelled nut or apple small.
The Jew plucked one. Like a fuzz-ball
It brake, discharging fetid dust.
"Pippins of Sodom? they've declined!"
Cried Derwent: "where's the ruddy rind?"
Said Rolfe: "If Circe tempt one thus,
A fig for vice—I'm virtuous.
Who but poor Margoth now would lust
After such fruitage. See, but see
What makes our Nehemiah to be
So strange. That look returns to him
Which late he wore by Achor's rim."

Over pale hollows foully smeared
The saint hung with an aspect weird:
"Yea, here it was the kings were tripped,
These, these the slime-pits where they slipped—
Gomorrah's lord and Sodom's, lo!"

"What's that?" asked Derwent.
"You should know,"
Said Rolfe: "your Scripture lore revive:
The four kings strove against the five
In Siddim here."
"Ah,—Genesis.
But turn; upon this other hand
See here another not remiss."
'Twas Margoth raking there the land.
Some minerals of noisome kind
He found and straight to pouch consigned.
"The chiffonier!" cried Rolfe; "e'en grim
Milcom and Chemosh scowl at him—
Here nosing underneath their lee
Of pagod hights."
In deeper dale
What canker may their palms assail?
Spotted they show, all limp they be.
Is it thy bitter mist, Bad Sea,
That, sudden driving, northward comes

Involving them, that each man roams
Half seen or lost?
But in the dark
Thick scud, the chanting saint they hark:
"Though through the valley of the shade
I pass, no evil do I fear;
His candle shineth on my head:
Lo he is with me. even here."

The rack drove by: and Derwent said—
"How apt he is!" then pause he made:
"This palm has grown a sorry sight;
A palm 'tis not, if named aright:
I'll drop it.—Look, the lake ahead!"

Canto XXIX - By the Marge

The legend round a Grecian urn,
The sylvan legend, though decay
Have wormed the garland all away,
And fire have left its Vandal burn;
Yet beauty inextinct may charm
In outline of the vessel's form.
Much so with Sodom, shore and sea.
Fair Como would like Sodom be
Should horror overrun the scene
And calcine all that makes it green,
Yet haply sparing to impeach
The contour in its larger reach.
In graceful lines the hills advance,

The valley's sweep repays the glance,
And wavy curves of winding beach;
But all is charred or crunched or riven,
Scarce seems of earth whereon we dwell;
Though framed within the lines of heaven
The picture intimates a hell.
That marge they win. Bides Mortmain there?
No trace of man, not anywhere.
It was the salt wave's northern brink.
No gravel bright nor shell was seen,
Nor kelpy growth nor coralline,
But dead boughs stranded, which the rout
Of Jordan, in old freshets born
In Libanus, had madly torn
Green from her arbor and thrust out

Into the liquid waste. No sound
Nor motion but of sea. The land
Was null: nor bramble, weed, nor trees,
Nor anything that grows on ground,
Flexile to indicate the breeze;
Though hitherward by south winds fanned
From Usdum's brink and Bozrah's site
Of bale, flew gritty atoms light.
Toward Karek's castle lost in blur,
And thence beyond toward Aroer
By Arnon where the robbers keep,
Jackal and vulture, eastward sweep
The waters, while their western rim
Stretches by Judah's headlands grim,
Which make in turns a sea-wall steep.
There, by the cliffs or distance hid,
The Fount or Cascade of the Kid
An Eden makes of one high glen,
One vernal and contrasted scene
In jaws of gloomy crags uncouth—
Rosemary in the black boar's mouth.
Alike withheld from present view
(And, until late, but hawk and kite
Visited the forgotten site),
The Maccabees' Masada true;
Stronghold which Flavian arms did rend,
The Peak of Eleazer's end,
Where patriot warriors made with brides
A martyrdom of suicides.
There too did Mariamne's hate
The death of John accelerate.
A crag of fairest, foulest weather—
Famous, and infamous together.
Hereof they spake, but never Vine,
Who little knew or seemed to know
Derived from books, but did incline
In docile way to each one's flow
Of knowledge bearing anyhow
In points less noted.
Southernmost
The sea indefinite was lost
Under a catafalque of cloud.
Unwelcome impress to disown
Or light evade, the priest, aloud
Taking an interested tone
And brisk, "Why, yonder lies Mount Hor,
E'en thereaway—that southward shore."
"Ay," added Rolfe, "and Aaron's cell

Thereon. A mountain sentinel,
He holds in solitude austere
The outpost of prohibited Seir
In cut-off Edom."
"God can sever!"
Brake in the saint, who nigh them stood;
"The satyr to the dragon's brood
Crieth! God's word abideth ever:
None there pass through—no, never, never!"
"My friend Max Levi, he passed through."
They turned. It was the hardy Jew.
Absorbed in vision here, the saint
Heard not. The priest in flushed constraint
Showed mixed emotion; part he winced
And part a humor pleased evinced—
Relish that would from qualms be free—
Aversion involved with sympathy.
But changing, and in formal way—
"Admitted; nay, 'tis tritely true;
Men pass thro' Edom, through and through.
But surely, few so dull to-day
As not to make allowance meet
For Orientalism's display
In Scripture, where the chapters treat
Of mystic themes."
With eye askance,
The apostate fixed no genial glance:
"Ay, Keith's grown obsolete. And, pray,
How long will these last glosses stay?
The agitating influence
Of knowledge never will dispense
With teasing faith, do what ye may.
Adjust and readjust, ye deal
With compass in a ship of steel."
"Such perturbations do but give
Proof that faith's vital: sensitive
Is faith, my friend."
"Go to, go to:
Your black bat! how she hangs askew,
Torpid, from wall by claws of wings:
Let drop the left—sticks fast the right;
Then this unhook—the other swings;
Leave—she regains her double plight."
"Ah, look," cried Derwent; "ah, behold!"
From the blue battlements of air,
Over saline vapors hovering there,
A flag was flung out—curved in fold—
Fiery, rosy, violet, green—

And, lovelier growing, brighter, fairer.
Transfigured all that evil scene;
And Iris was the standard-bearer.
None spake. As in a world made new,
With upturned faces they review
That oriflamme, the which no man
Would look for in such clime of ban.
'Twas northern; and its home-like look
Touched Nehemiah. He, late with book
Gliding from Margoth's dubious sway,
Was standing by the ass apart;
And when he caught that scarf of May
How many a year ran back his heart:
Scythes hang in orchard, hay-cocks loom
After eve-showers, the mossed roofs gloom
Greenly beneath the homestead trees;
He tingles with these memories.
For Vine, over him suffusive stole
An efflorescence; all the soul
Flowering in flush upon the brow.
But 'twas ambiguously replaced
In words addressed to Clarel now—
"Yonder the arch dips in the waste;
Thither! and win the pouch of gold."
Derwent reproached him: "ah, withhold!
See, even death's pool reflects the dyes—
The rose upon the coffin lies!"
"Brave words," said Margoth, plodding near;
"Brave words; but yonder bow's forsworn.
The covenant made on Noah's morn,
Was that well kept? why, hardly here,
Where whelmed by fire and flood, they say,
The townsfolk sank in after day,
Yon sign in heaven should reappear."
They heard, but in such torpid gloom
Scarcely they recked, for now the bloom
Vanished from sight, and half the sea
Died down to glazed monotony.
Craved solace here would Clarel prove,
Recalling Ruth, her glance of love.
But nay; those eyes so frequent known
To meet, and mellow on his own—
Now, in his vision of them, swerved;
While in perverse recurrence ran
Dreams of the bier Armenian.

Against their sway his soul he nerved:
"Go, goblins; go, each funeral thought—

Bewitchment from this Dead Sea caught!"

Westward they move, and turn the shore
Southward, till, where wild rocks are set,
Dismounting, they would fain restore
Ease to the limb. But haunts them yet
A dumb dejection lately met.

Canto XXX - Of Petra

"The City Red in cloud-land lies
Yonder," said Derwent, quick to inter
The ill, or light regard transfer:
"But Petra must we leave unseen—
Tell us"—to Rolfe "there hast thou been."
"With dragons guarded roundabout
'Twas a new Jason found her out—
Burckhardt, you know." "But tell." "The flume
Or mountain corridor profound
Whereby ye win the inner ground
Petraean; this, from purple gloom
Of cliffs—whose tops the suns illume
Where oleanders wave the flag—
Winds out upon the rosy stain,
Warm color of the natural vein,
Of porch and pediment in crag.
One starts. In Esau's waste are blent
Ionian form, Venetian tint.
Statues salute ye from that fane,
The warders of the Horite lane.
They welcome, seem to point ye on
Where sequels which transcend them dwell;
But tarry, for just here is won
Happy suspension of the spell."
"But expectation's raised."
"No more!
'Tis then when bluely blurred in shore,
It looms through azure haze at sea—
Then most 'tis Colchis charmeth ye.
So ever, and with all! But, come,
Imagine us now quite at home
Taking the prospect from Mount Hor.
Good. Eastward turn thee skipping o'er
The intervening craggy blight:
Mark'st thou the face of yon slabbed hight
Shouldered about by hights? what Door

Is that, sculptured in elfin freak?
The portal of the Prince o' the Air?
Thence will the god emerge, and speak?
El Deir it is; and Petra's there,
Down in her cleft. Mid such a scene
Of Nature's terror, how serene
That ordered form. Nor less 'tis cut
Out of that terror—does abut
Thereon: there's Art."
"Dare say—no doubt;
But, prithee, turn we now about
And closer get thereto in mind;
That portal lures me."
"Nay, forbear;
A bootless journey. We should wind
Along ravine by mountain-stair,—
Down which in season torrents sweep—
Up, slant by sepulchers in steep,
Grotto and porch, and so get near
Puck's platform, and thereby El Deir.
We'd knock. An echo. Knock again—
Ay, knock forever: none requite:
The live spring filters through cell, fane,
And tomb: a dream the Edomite!"
"And dreamers all who dream of him—
Though Sinbad's pleasant in the skim.
Paestum and Petra: good to use
For sedative when one would muse.

But look, our Emir.—Ay, Djalea,
We guess why thou com'st mutely here
And hintful stand'st before us so."
"Ay, ay," said Rolfe; "stirrups, and go!"
"But first," the priest said, "let me creep
And rouse our poor friend slumbering low
Under yon rock—queer place to sleep."

"Queer?" muttered Rolfe as Derwent went;
"Queer is the furthest he will go
In phrase of a disparagement.
But—ominous, with haggard rent—
To me yon crag's brow-beating brow
Looks horrible—and I say so."

Canto XXXI - The Inscription

While yet Rolfe's foot in stirrup stood,
Ere the light vault that wins the seat,
Derwent was heard: "What's this we meet?
A Cross? and—if one could but spell—
Inscription Sinaitic? Well,
Mortmain is nigh—his crazy freak;
Whose else? A closer view I'll seek;
I'll climb."

In moving there aside
The rock's turned brow he had espied;
In rear this rock hung o'er the waste
And Nehemiah in sleep embraced
Below. The forepart gloomed Lot's wave
So nigh, the tide the base did lave.
Above, the sea-face smooth was worn
Through long attrition of that grit
Which on the waste of winds is borne.
And on the tablet high of it—
Traced in dull chalk, such as is found
Accessible in upper ground—
Big there between two scrawls, below
And over—a cross; three stars in row
Upright, two more for thwarting limb
Which drooped oblique.
At Derwent's cry
The rest drew near; and every eye
Marked the device.—Thy passion's whim,
Wild Swede, mused Vine in silent heart.
"Looks like the Southern Cross to me,"
Said Clarel; "so 'tis down in chart."
"And so," said Rolfe, "'tis set in sky—
Though error slight of place prevail
In midmost star here chalked. At sea,
Bound for Peru, when south ye sail,
Startling that novel cluster strange
Peers up from low; then as ye range
Cape-ward still further, brightly higher
And higher the stranger doth aspire,
'Till off the Horn, when at full hight
Ye slack your gaze as chilly grows the night.
But Derwent—see!"
The priest having gained
Convenient lodge the text below,
They called: "What's that in curve contained
Above the stars? Read: we would know."
"Runs thus: By one who wails the loss,
This altar to the Slanting Cross."

"Ha! under that?" "Some crow's-foot scrawl."
"Decipher, quick! we're waiting all."
"Patience: for ere one try rehearse,
'Twere well to make it out. 'Tis verse."
"Verse, say you? Read." "'Tis mystical:
"'Emblazoned bleak in austral skies—
A heaven remote, whose starry swarm
Like Science lights but cannot warm—
Translated Cross, hast thou withdrawn,
Dim paling too at every dawn,
With symbols vain once counted wise,
And gods declined to heraldries?
Estranged, estranged: can friend prove so?

Aloft, aloof, a frigid sign:
How far removed, thou Tree divine,
Whose tender fruit did reach so low—
Love apples of New-Paradise!
About the wide Australian sea
The planted nations yet to be
When, ages hence, they lift their eyes,
Tell, what shall they retain of thee?
But class thee with Orion's sword?
In constellations unadored,
Christ and the Giant equal prize?
The atheist cycles—must they be?
Fomentors as forefathers we?'

"Mad, mad enough," the priest here cried,
Down slipping by the shelving brinks;
"But 'tis not Mortmain," and he sighed.
"Not Mortmain?" Rolfe exclaimed. "Methinks,"
The priest, "'tis hardly in his vein."
"How? fraught with feeling is the strain?
His heart's not ballasted with stone—
He's crank." "Well, well, e'en let us own
That Mortmain, Mortmain is the man.
We've then a pledge here at a glance
Our comrade's met with no mischance.

Soon he'll rejoin us." "There, amen!"
"But now to wake Nehemiah in den
Behind here.—But kind Clarel goes.
Strange how he naps nor trouble knows
Under the crag's impending block,
Nor fears its fall, nor recks of shock."

Anon they mount; and much advance

Upon that chalked significance.
The student harks, and weighs each word,
Intent, he being newly stirred.

But tarries Margoth? Yes, behind
He lingers. He placards his mind:
Scaling the crag he rudely scores
With the same chalk (how here abused!)
Left by the other, after used,
A sledge or hammer huge as Thor's;
A legend lending—this, to wit:
"I, Science, I whose gain's thy loss,
I slanted thee, thou Slanting Cross."
But sun and rain, and wind, with grit
Driving, these haste to cancel it.

Canto XXXII - The Encampment

Southward they find a strip at need
Between the mount and marge, and make,
In expectation of the Swede,
Encampment there, nor shun the Lake.
'Twas afternoon. With Arab zest
The Bethlehemites their spears present,
Whereon they lift and spread the tent
And care for all.
As Rolfe from rest
Came out, toward early eventide,
His comrades sat the shore beside,
In shadow deep, which from the west
The main Judaean mountains flung.
That ridge they faced, and anxious hung
Awaiting Mortmain, some having grown
The more concerned, because from stone
Inscribed, they had indulged a hope:
But now in ill surmise they grope.
Anew they question grave Djalea.
But what knows he?
Their hearts to cheer,
'Trust," Derwent said, "hope's silver bell;
Nor dream he'd do his life a wrong—
No, never!"
"Demons here which dwell,"
Cried Rolfe, "riff-raff of Satan's throng,
May fetch him steel, rope, poison—well,
He'd spurn them, hoot their scurvy hell:

There's nobler.—But what other knell
Of hap—" He turned him toward the sea.
Like leagues of ice which slumberous roll
About the pivot of the pole—
Vitreous—glass it seemed to be.
Beyond, removed in air sublime,
As 'twere some more than human clime,
In flanking towers of AEtna hue
The Ammonitish mounts they view
Enkindled by the sunset cast
Over Judah's ridgy headlands massed
Which blacken baseward. Ranging higher
Where vague glens pierced the steeps of fire,
Imagination time repealed—
Restored there, and in fear revealed
Lot and his daughters twain in flight,
Three shadows flung on reflex light
Of Sodom in her funeral pyre.
Some fed upon the natural scene,
Deriving many a wandering hint
Such as will oft times intervene
When on the slab ye view the print
Of perished species.—Judge Rolfe's start
And quick revulsion, when, apart,
Derwent he saw at ease reclined,
With page before him, page refined
And appetizing, which threw ope
New parks, fresh walks for Signor Hope
To saunter in.
"And read you here?
Scarce suits the ground with bookish cheer.
Escaped from forms, enlarged at last,
Pupils we be of wave and waste—
Not books; nay, nay!"
"Book-comment, though,"—
Smiled Derwent—"were it ill to know?"
"But how if nature vetoes all
Her commentators? Disenthrall
Thy heart. Look round. Are not here met
Books and that truth no type shall set?"—
Then, to himself in refluent flow:
"Earnest again!—well, let it go."
Derwent quick glanced from face to face,
Lighting upon the student's hue
Of pale perplexity, with trace
Almost of twinge at Rolfe: "Believe,
Though here I random page review,
Not books I let exclusive cleave

And sway. Much too there is, I grant,
Which well might Solomon's wisdom daunt—
Much that we mark. Nevertheless,
Were it a paradox to confess
A book's a man? If this be so,
Books be but part of nature. Oh,
'Tis studying nature, reading books:
And 'tis through Nature each heart looks
Up to a God, or whatsoe'er
One images beyond our sphere.
Moreover, Siddim's not the world:
There's Naples. Why, yourself well know
What breadths of beauty lie unfurled
All round the bays where sailors go.
So, prithee, do not be severe,
But let me read."
Rolfe looked esteem:
"You suave St. Francis! Him, I mean,
Of Sales, not that soul whose dream
Founded the bare-foot Order lean.
Though wise as serpents, Sales proves
The throbbings sweet of social doves.
I like you. "
Derwent laughed; then, "Ah,
From each Saint Francis am I far!"
And grave he grew.
It was a scene
Which Clarel in his memory scored:
How reconcile Rolfe's wizard chord
And forks of esoteric fire,
With common-place of laxer mien?
May truth be such a spendthrift lord?
Then Derwent: he reviewed in heart
His tone with Margoth; his attire
Of tolerance; the easy part
He played. Could Derwent, having gained
A certain slant in liberal thought,
Think there to bide, like one detained
Half-way adown the slippery glacier caught?
Was honesty his, with lore and art
Not to be fooled?—But if in vain
One tries to comprehend a man,
How think to sound God's deeper heart!

Canto XXXIII - Lot's Sea

Roving along the winding verge
Trying these problems as a lock,
Clarel upon the further marge
Caught sight of Vine. Upon a rock
LOW couchant there, and dumb as that,
Bent on the wave Vine moveless sat.
The student after pause drew near:
Then, as in presence which though mute
Did not repel, without salute
He joined him.
         Unto these, by chance
In ruminating slow advance
Came Rolfe, and lingered.
         At Vine's feet
A branchless tree lay lodged ashore,
One end immersed. Of form complete
Half fossilized—could this have been,
In ages back, a palm-shaft green?
Yes, long detained in depths which store
A bitter virtue, there it lay,
Washed up to sight—free from decay
But dead.
         And now in slouched return
From random prowlings, brief sojourn
As chance might prompt, the Jew they espy
Coasting inquisitive the shore
And frequent stooping. Ranging nigh,
In hirsute hand a flint he bore
A flint, or stone, of smooth dull gloom:
"A jewel? not asphaltum—no:
Observe it, pray. Methinks in show
'Tis like the flagging round that Tomb
Ye celebrate."
         Rolfe, glancing, said,
"I err, or 'twas from Siddim's bed
Or quarry here, those floor-stones came:
'Tis Stone-of-Moses called, they vouch;
The Arabs know it by that name."
"Moses? who's Moses?" Into pouch
The lump he slipped; while wistful here
Clarel in silence challenged Vine;
But not responsive was Vine's cheer,
Discharged of every meaning sign.
With motive, Rolfe the talk renewed:
"Yes, here it was the cities stood
That sank in reprobation. See,
The scene and record well agree."
"Tut, tut—tut, tut. Of aqueous force,

Vent igneous, a shake or so,
One here perceives the sign—of course;
All's mere geology, you know."
"Nay, how should one know that?"
"By sight,
Touch, taste—all senses in assent
Of common sense their parliament.
Judge now; this lake, with outlet none
And into which five streams discharge
From south; which east and west is shown
Walled in by Alps along the marge;
North. in this lake. the waters end
Of Jordan end here, or dilate
Rather, and so evaporate
From surface. But do you attend?"
"Most teachably."
"Well, now: assume
This lake was formed, even as they tell,
Then first when the Five Cities fell;
Where, I demand, ere yet that doom,
Where emptied Jordan?"
"Who can say?
Not I.
"No, none. A point I make:
Coeval are the stream and lake!
I say no more."
As came that close
A hideous hee-haw horrible rose,
Rebounded in unearthly sort
From shore to shore, as if retort
From all the damned in Sodom's Sea
Out brayed at him. "Just God, what's that?"
"The ass," breathed Vine, with tropic eye
Freakishly impish, nor less shy;
Then, distant as before, he sat.
Anew Rolfe turned toward Margoth then;
"May not these levels high and low
Have undergone derangement when
The cities met their overthrow?
Or say there was a lake at first—
A supposition not reversed
By Writ—a lake enlarged through doom
Which overtook the cities? Come!"—
The Jew, recovering from decline
Arising from late asinine
Applause, replied hereto in way
Eliciting from Rolfe—"Delay:
What knowest thou? or what know I?

Suspect you may ere yet you die
Or afterward perchance may learn,
That Moses' God is no mere Pam
With painted clubs, but true I AM."
"Hog-Latin," was the quick return;
"Plague on that ass!" for here again
Brake in the pestilent refrain.
Meanwhile, as if in a dissent
Not bordering their element,
Vine kept his place, aloof in air.
They could but part and leave him there;
The Hebrew railing as they went—
"Of all the dolorous dull men!
He's like a poor nun's pining hen.
And me too: should I let it pass?
Ass? did he say it was the ass?"
Hereat, timed like the clerk's Amen
Yet once more did the hee-haw free
Come in with new alacrity.

Vine tarried; and with fitful hand
Took bits of dead drift from the sand
And flung them to the wave, as one
Whose race of thought long since was run—
For whom the spots enlarge that blot the golden sun.

XXXIV - Mortmain Reappears

While now at poise the wings of shade
Outstretched overhang each ridge and glade,
Mortmain descends from Judah's hight
Through sally-port of minor glens:
Against the background of black dens
Blacker the figure glooms enhanced.
Relieved from anxious fears, the group
In friendliness would have advanced
To greet, but shrank or fell adroop.
Like Hecla ice inveined with marl
And frozen cinders showed his face
Rigid and darkened. Shunning parle
He seated him aloof in place,
Hands clasped about the knees drawn up
As round the cask the binding hoop—
Condensed in self, or like a seer
Unconscious of each object near,
While yet, informed, the nerve may reach

Like wire under wave to furthest beach.
By what brook Cherith had he been,
Watching it shrivel from the scene—
Or voice aerial had heard,
That now he murmured the wild word;
"But, hectored by the impious years,
What god invoke, for leave to unveil
That gulf whither tend these modern fears,
And deeps over which men crowd the sail?"
Up, as possessed, he rose anon,
And crying to the beach went down:
"Repent! repent in every land
Or hell's hot kingdom is at hand!
Yea, yea,
In pause of the artillery's boom,
While now the armed world holds its own,
The comet peers, the star dips down;
Flicker the lamps in Syria's tomb,
While Anti-Christ and Atheist set
On Anarch the red coronet!"

"MadJohn," sighed Rolfe, "dost there betray
The dire Vox Clamans of our day?"
"Why heed him?" Derwent breathed: "alas!
Let him alone, and it will pass.—
What would he now?" Before the bay
Low bowed he there, with hand addressed
To scoop. "Unhappy, hadst thou best?"
Djalea it was; then calling low
Unto a Bethlehemite whose brow
Was wrinkled like the bat's shrunk hide
"Your salt-song, Beltha: warn and chide."

"Would ye know what bitter drink
They gave to Christ upon the Tree?
Sip the wave that laps the brink
Of Siddim: taste, and God keep ye!
It drains the hills where alum's hid—
Drains the rock-salt's ancient bed;
Hither unto basin fall
The torrents from the steeps of gall—
Here is Hades' water-shed.
Sinner, would ye that your soul
Bitter were and like the pool?
Sip the Sodom waters dead;
But never from thy heart shall haste
The Marah—yea, the after-taste."

He closed.—Arrested as he stooped,
Did Mortmain his pale hand recall?
No; undeterred the wave he scooped,
And tried it—madly tried the gall.

Canto XXXV - Prelusive

In Piranesi's rarer prints,
Interiors measurelessly strange,
Where the distrustful thought may range
Misgiving still—what mean the hints?
Stairs upon stairs which dim ascend
In series from plunged Bastiles drear—
Pit under pit; long tier on tier
Of shadowed galleries which impend
Over cloisters, cloisters without end;
The hight, the depth—the far, the near;
Ring-bolts to pillars in vaulted lanes,
And dragging Rhadamanthine chains;
These less of wizard influence lend
Than some allusive chambers closed.
Those wards of hush are not disposed
In gibe of goblin fantasy—
Grimace unclean diablery:
Thy wings, Imagination, span
Ideal truth in fable's seat:
The thing implied is one with man,
His penetralia of retreat—
The heart, with labyrinths replete:
In freaks of intimation see
Paul's "mystery of iniquity:"
Involved indeed, a blur of dream;
As, awed by scruple and restricted
In first design, or interdicted
By fate and warnings as might seem;
The inventor miraged all the maze,
Obscured it with prudential haze;
Nor less, if subject unto question,
The egg left, egg of the suggestion.
Dwell on those etchings in the night,
Those touches bitten in the steel
By aqua-fortis, till ye feel
The Pauline text in gray of light;
Turn hither then and read aright.

For ye who green or gray retain

Childhood's illusion, or but feign;
As bride and suit let pass a bier—
So pass the coming canto here.

Canto XXXVI - Sodom

Full night. The moon has yet to rise;
The air oppresses, and the skies
Reveal beyond the lake afar
One solitary tawny star—
Complexioned so by vapors dim,
Whereof some hang above the brim
And nearer waters of the lake,
Whose bubbling air-beads mount and break
As charged with breath of things alive.

In talk about the Cities Five
Engulfed, on beach they linger late.
And he, the quaffer of the brine,
Puckered with that heart-wizening wine
Of bitterness, among them sate
Upon a camel's skull, late dragged
From forth the wave, the eye-pits slagged
With crusted salt.—"What star is yon?"
And pointed to that single one
Befogged above the sea afar.
"It might be Mars, so red it shines,"
One answered; "duskily it pines
In this strange mist."—"It is the star
Called Wormwood. Some hearts die in thrall
Of waters which yon star makes gall;"
And, lapsing, turned, and made review
Of what that wickedness might be
Which down on these ill precincts drew
The flood, the fire; put forth new plea,
Which not with Writ might disagree;
Urged that those malefactors stood
Guilty of sins scarce scored as crimes
In any statute known, or code—
Nor now, nor in the former times:
Things hard to prove: decorum's wile,
Malice discreet, judicious guile;
Good done with ill intent—reversed:
Best deeds designed to serve the worst;
And hate which under life's fair hue
Prowls like the shark in sunned Pacific blue.

He paused, and under stress did bow,
Lank hands enlocked across the brow.
"Nay, nay, thou sea,
'Twas not all carnal harlotry,
But sins refined, crimes of the spirit,
Helped earn that doom ye here inherit:
Doom well imposed, though sharp and dread,
In some god's reign, some god long fled.—
Thou gaseous puff of mineral breath
Mephitical; thou swooning flaw
That fann'st me from this pond of death;

Wert thou that venomous small thing
Which tickled with the poisoned straw?
Thou, stronger, but who yet couldst start
Shrinking with sympathetic sting,
While willing the uncompunctious dart!
Ah, ghosts of Sodom, how ye thrill
About me in this peccant air,
Conjuring yet to spare, but spare!
Fie, fie, that didst in formal will
Plot piously the posthumous snare.
And thou, the mud-flow—evil mass
Of surest-footed sluggishness
Swamping the nobler breed—art there?
Moan, Burker of kind heart: all's known
To Him; with thy connivers, moan.—
Sinners—expelled, transmuted souls
Blown in these airs, or whirled in shoals
Of gurgles which your gasps send up,
Or on this crater marge and cup
Slavered in slime, or puffed in stench—
Not ever on the tavern bench
Ye lolled. Few dicers here, few sots,
Few sluggards, and no idiots.
'Tis thou who servedst Mammon's hate
Or greed through forms which holy are—
Black slaver steering by a star,
'Tis thou—and all like thee in state.
Who knew the world, yet varnished it;
Who traded on the coast of crime
Though landing not; who did outwit
Justice, his brother, and the time—
These, chiefly these, to doom submit.
But who the manifold may tell?
And sins there be inserutable,
Unutterable. "
Ending there

He shrank, and like an osprey gray
Peered on the wave. His hollow stare
Marked then some smaller bubbles play
In cluster silvery like spray:
"Be these the beads on the wives'-wine,
Tofana-brew?—O fair Medea—
O soft man-eater, furry-fine:
Oh, be thou Jael, be thou Leah—
Unfathomably shallow!—No!
Nearer the core than man can go
Or Science get—nearer the slime
Of nature's rudiments and lime
In chyle before the bone. Thee, thee,
In thee the filmy cell is spun—
The mould thou art of what men be:
Events are all in thee begun—
By thee, through thee!—Undo, undo,
Prithee, undo, and still renew
The fall forever!"
On his throne
He lapsed; and muffled came the moan
How multitudinous in sound,
From Sodom's wave. He glanced around:
They all had left him, one by one.
Was it because he open threw
The inmost to the outward view?
Or did but pain at frenzied thought,
Prompt to avoid him, since but naught
In such case might remonstrance do?
But none there ventured idle plea,
Weak sneer, or fraudful levity.

Two spirits, hovering in remove,
Sad with inefficacious love,
Here sighed debate: "Ah, Zoima, say;
Be it far from me to impute a sin,
But may a sinless nature win
Those deeps he knows?"—"Sin shuns that way;
Sin acts the sin, but flees the thought
That sweeps the abyss that sin has wrought.
Innocent be the heart and true—
Howe'er it feed on bitter bread—
That, venturous through the Evil led,
Moves as along the ocean's bed
Amid the dragon's staring crew."

Canto XXXVII - Of Traditions

Credit the Arab wizard lean,
And still at favoring hour are seen
(But not by Franks, whom doubts debar)
Through waves the cities overthrown:
Seboym and Segor, Aldemah,
With two whereof the foul renown
And syllables more widely reign.
Astarte, worshiped on the Plain
Ere Terah's day, her vigil keeps
Devoted where her temple sleeps
Like moss within the agate's vein—
A ruin in the lucid sea.
The columns lie overlappingly—
Slant, as in order smooth they slid
Down the live slope. Her ray can bid
Their beauty thrill along the lane
Of tremulous silver. By the marge
(If yet the Arab credence gain)
At slack wave, when midsummer's glow
Widens the shallows, statues show—
He vouches; and will more enlarge
On sculptured basins broad in span,
With alum scurfed and alkatran.
Nay, further—let who will, believe—
As monks aver, on holy eve,
Easter or John's, along the strand
Shadows Corinthian wiles inweave:
Voluptuous palaces expand,
From whose moon-lighted colonnade
Beckons Armida, deadly maid:
Traditions; and their fountains run
Beyond King Nine and Babylon.

But disenchanters grave maintain
That in the time ere Sodom's fall
'Twas shepherds here endured life's pain:
Shepherds, and all was pastoral
In Siddim; Abraham and Lot,
Blanketed Bedouins of the plain;
Sodom and her four daughters small—
For Sodom held maternal reign—
Poor little hamlets, such as dot
The mountain side and valley way
Of Syria as she shows to-day;
The East, where constancies indwell,
Such hint may give: 'tis plausible.

Hereof the group—from Mortmain's blight
Withdrawn where sands the beach embayed
And Nehemiah apart was laid—
Held curious discourse that night.
They chatted; but 'twas underrun
By heavier current. And anon,
After the meek one had retired
Under the tent, the thought transpired,
And Mortmain was the theme.
"If mad,
'Tis indignation at the bad,"
Said Rolfe; "most men somehow get used
To seeing evil, though not all
They see; 'tis sympathetical;
But never some are disabused
Of first impressions which appal."
"There, there," cried Derwent, "let it fall.
Assume that some are but so-so,
They'll be transfigured. Let suffice:
Dismas he dwells in Paradise."
"Who?" "Dismas the Good Thief, you know.
Ay, and the Blest One shared the cup
WithJudas; e'en letJudas sup
With him, at the Last Supper too.—
But see!"

It was the busy Jew
With chemic lamp aflame, by tent
Trying some shrewd experiment
With minerals secured that day,
Dead unctuous stones.
"Look how his ray,"
Said Rolfe, "too small for stars to heed,
Strange lights him, reason's sorcerer,
Poor Simon Magus run to seed.
And, yes, 'twas here—or else I err—
The legends claim, that into sea
The old magician flung his book
When life and lore he both forsook:
The evil spell yet lurks, may be.—
But yon strange orb—can be the moon?
These vapors: and the waters swoon."

Ere long the tent received them all;
They slumber—wait the morning's call.

Now Nehemiah with wistful heart
Much heed had given to myths which bore
Upon that Pentateuchal shore;
Him could the wilder legend thrill
With credulous impulse, whose appeal,
Oblique, touched on his Christian vein.
Wakeful he bode. With throbbing brain
O'erwrought by travel, long he lay
In febrile musings, life's decay,
Begetting soon an ecstasy
Wherein he saw arcade and fane
And people moving in the deep;
Strange hum he heard, and minstrel-sweep.
Then, by that sleight each dreamer knows,
Dream merged in dream: the city rose—
Shrouded, it went up from the wave;
Transfigured came down out of heaven
Clad like a bride in splendor brave.
There, through the streets, with purling sound
Clear waters the clear agates lave,
Opal and pearl in pebbles strown;
The palaces with palms were crowned—
The water-palaces each one;
And from the fount of rivers shone
Soft rays as of Saint Martin's sun;
Last, dearer than ere Jason found,
A fleece—the Fleece upon a throne!
And a great voice he hears which saith,
Pain is no more, no more is death;
I wipe away all tears: Come, ye,
Enter, it is eternity.
And happy souls, the saved and blest,
Welcomed by angels and caressed,
Hand linked in hand like lovers sweet,
Festoons of tenderness complete—
Roamed up and on, by orchards fair
To bright ascents and mellower air;
Thence, highest, toward the throne were led,
And kissed, amid the sobbings shed
Of faith fulfilled.—In magic play
So to the meek one in the dream
Appeared the New Jerusalem:
Haven for which how many a day—
In bed, afoot, or on the knee
He yearned: Would God I were in thee!

The visions changed and counterchanged—
Blended and parted—distant ranged,
And beckoned, beckoned him away.
In sleep he rose; and none did wist
When vanished this somnambulist.

Canto XXXIX - Obsequies

The camel's skull upon the beach
No more the sluggish waters reach—
No more the languid waters lave;
Not now they wander in and out
Of those void chambers walled about—
So dull the calm, so dead the wave.
Above thick mist how pallid looms,
While the slurred day doth wanly break,
Ammon's long ridge beyond the lake.

Down to the shrouded margin comes
Lone Vine and starts: not at the skull,
The camel's, for that bides the same
As when overnight 'twas Mortmain's stool.
But, nigh it—how that object name?
Slant on the shore, ground-curls of mist
Enfold it, as in amethyst
Subdued, small flames in dead of night
Lick the dumb back-log ashy white.
What is it?—paler than the pale
Pervading vapors, which so veil,
That some peak-tops are islanded
Baseless above the dull, dull bed
Of waters, which not e'en transmit
One ripple 'gainst the cheek of It.

The start which the discoverer gave
Was physical—scarce shocked the soul,

Since many a prior revery grave
Forearmed against alarm's control.
To him, indeed, each lapse and end
Meet—in harmonious method blend.
Lowly he murmured, "Here is balm:
Repose is snowed upon repose—
Sleep upon sleep; it is the calm
And incantation of the close."

The others, summoned to the spot,
Were staggered: Nehemiah? no!
The innocent and sinless—what!—
Pale lying like the Assyrian low?

The Swede stood by; nor after-taste
Extinct was of the liquid waste
Nor influence of that Wormwood Star
Whereof he spake. All overcast—
His genial spirits meeting jar—
Derwent on no unfeeling plea
Held back. Mortmain, relentless: "See:
To view death on the bed—at ease—
A dream, and draped; to minister
To inheriting kin; to comfort these
In chamber comfortable;—here
The elements all that unsay!
The first man dies. Thus Abel lay."
The sad priest, rightly to be read
Scarce hoping,—pained, dispirited—
Was dumb. And Mortmain went aside
In thrill by only Vine espied:
Alas (thought Vine) thou bitter Swede,
Into thine armor dost thou bleed?

Intent but poised, the Druze looked on:
"The sheath: the sword?"
"Ah, whither gone?"
Clarel, and bowed him there and kneeled:
"Whither art gone? thou friendliest mind
Unfriended—what friend now shalt find?
Robin or raven, hath God a bird
To come and strew thee, lone interred,
With leaves, when here left far behind?"
"He's gone," the Jew; "czars, stars must go
Or change! All's chymestry. Aye so."—
"Resurget"—faintly Derwent there.
"In pace"—Vine, nor more would dare.

Rolfe in his reaching heart did win
Prelude remote, yet gathering in:
"Moist, moist with sobs and balsam shed—
Warm tears, cold odors from the urn—
They hearsed in heathen Rome their dead
Nor hopeful of the soul's return.
-Embracing them, in marble set,
' The mimic gates of Orcus met—
The Pluto-bolt, the fatal one

Wreathed over by the hung festoon.
How fare we now? But were it clear
In nature or in lore devout
That parted souls live on in cheer,
Gladness would be shut pathos out.
His poor thin life: the end? no more?
The end here by the Dead Sea shore?"
He turned him, as awaiting nod
Or answer from earth, air, or skies;
But be it ether or the clod,
The elements yield no replies.
Cross-legged on a cindery hight,
Belex, the fatalist, smoked on.
Slow whiffs; and then, "It needs be done:
Come, beach the loins there, Bethlehemite."—
Inside a hollow free from stone
With camel-ribs they scooped a trench;
And Derwent, rallying from blench
Of Mortmain's brow, and nothing loth
Tacit to vindicate the cloth,
Craved they would bring to him the Book,
Now ownerless. The same he took,
And thence had culled brief service meet,
But closed, reminded of the psalm
Heard when the salt fog shrunk the palm—
They wending toward these waters' seat—
Raised by the saint, as e'en it lent
A voice to low presentiment:
Naught better might one here repeat:
"Though through the valley of the shade
I pass, no evil do I fear;
His candle shineth on my head:
Lo, he is with me, even here. "

That o'er, they kneeled—with foreheads bare
Bowed as he made the burial prayer.
Even Margoth bent him; but 'twas so
As some hard salt at sea will do
Holding the narrow plank that bears
The shotted hammock, while brief prayers
Are by the master read mid war
Relentless of wild elements—
The sleet congealing on the spar:
It was a sulking reverence.
The body now the Arabs placed
Within the grave, and then with haste
Had covered, but for Rolfe's restraint:
"The Book!"—The Bible of the saint—

With that the relics there he graced,
Yea, put it in the hand: "Since now
The last long journey thou dost go,
Why part thee from thy friend and guide!
And better guide who knoweth? Bide."

They closed. And came a rush, a roar—
Aloof, but growing more and more,
Nearer and nearer. They invoke
The long Judaic range, the hight
Of nearer mountains hid from sight
By the blind mist. Nor spark nor smoke
Of that plunged wake their eyes might see;
But, hoarse in hubbub, horribly,
With all its retinue around—
Flints, dust, and showers of splintered stone,
An avalanche of rock down tore,
In somerset from each rebound—
Thud upon thump—down, down and down—
And landed. Lull. Then shore to shore
Rolled the deep echo, fold on fold,
Which, so reverberated, bowled
And bowled far down the long El Ghor.

They turn; and, in that silence sealed,
What works there from behind the veil?
A counter object is revealed—
A thing of heaven, and yet how frail:
Up in thin mist above the sea
Humid is formed, and noiselessly,
The fog-bow: segment of an oval
Set in a colorless removal
Against a vertical shaft, or slight
Slim pencil of an aqueous light.
Suspended there, the segment hung
Like to the May-wreath that is swung
Against the pole. It showed half spent—
Hovered and trembled, paled away, and—went.

END OF SECOND PART

Herman Melville – A Short Biography

Herman Melville was born in New York City on August 1st, 1819, the third of eight children.

At the age of 7 Melville contracted scarlet fever which was to permanently diminish his eyesight. At this time Melville was described as being "very backwards in speech and somewhat slow in comprehension."

Melville attended the Albany Academy from October 1830 to October 1831, where he took the standard preparatory course; reading and spelling; penmanship; arithmetic; English grammar; geography; natural history; universal, Greek, Roman and English history; classical biography; and Jewish antiquities.

The reasons for Melville leaving the Academy after a year are unknown although his brothers continued their education there for a few more months.

In December, Melville's father returned from New York City by steamboat, but difficult weather forced him to travel the last 70 miles in an open carriage in freezing temperatures. A cold developed into delirium and by January 28th, not yet fifty, his father was dead. Melville, at home by now, most probably witnessed much of this event and two decades later he described scenes that must have been very similar in the death of Pierre's father in Pierre.

The family were now in very straitened times. Just 14 Melville took a job in a bank paying $150 a year that he obtained via his uncle, Peter Gansevoort, who was one of the directors of the New York State Bank.

Melville was briefly able to attend again the Albany Academy from October 1836 to March 1837, where he studied the classics.

After a failed stint as a surveyor he signed on to go to sea and travelled across the Atlantic to Liverpool and then on further voyages to the Pacific on adventures which would soon become the architecture of his novels. Whilst travelling he joined a mutiny, was jailed, fell in love with a South Pacific beauty and became known as a figure of opposition to the coercion of native Hawaiians to the Christian religion.

He drew from these experiences in his books Typee, Omoo, and White-Jacket. These were published as novels, the first initially in London in 1846.

They sold very well and enabled him to write full time although royalties were not vast. (During his career it is estimated his writing brought him no more than $10,000)

After a three-month courtship of Elizabeth Shaw, daughter of a prominent Boston family, her father was the Chief Justice of the Massachusetts Supreme Judicial Court, they decided to marry. Her father initially turned down Melville's request but on August 14th, 1847 they married. After initially settling in New York they moved to Massachusetts.

In September of 1850, Melville borrowed $3,000 from his father-in-law Lemuel Shaw to buy a 160-acre farm in Pittsfield. Melville christened the new home 'Arrowhead', due to the quantity of arrowheads dug up around the property during planting season.

That winter, Melville on an impulse paid a visit to the writer Nathaniel Hawthorne. At the time Hawthorne was finishing The House of the Seven Gables and "not in the mood for company". Hawthorne's wife Sophia entertained him while he waited for Hawthorne to come down for supper, and gave him copies of Twice-Told Tales and, The Grandfather's Chair. Melville, sensing a friendship developing, invited them to Arrowhead during the coming weeks. When Sophia agreed, he looked forward to "discussing the Universe with a bottle of brandy & cigars" with Hawthorne.

By 1851 his masterpiece, Moby Dick, was ready to be published. It is perhaps, and certainly at the time, one of the most ambitious novels ever written. However, it never sold out its initial print run of 3,000 and Melville's earnings on this masterpiece were a mere $556.37.

In succeeding years his reputation waned and he found life increasingly difficult. His family was growing, now four children, and a stable income was essential.

From 1853 to 1856, Melville began to publish his short stories in the growing magazine market, most notably "Bartleby, the Scrivener" (1853), "The Encantadas" (1854), and "Benito Cereno" (1855). These and others were later collected together and published in 1856 as the Plazza Tales.

In 1857, he travelled to England where, for the first time since 1852, he reunited with Hawthorne. He then went on to tour the Near East. The Confidence-Man was the last prose work that he published that same year. It received little attention.

With his finances in a disappointing state Melville took the advice of friends that a change in career was called for. For many others public lecturing had proved very rewarding. From late 1857 to 1860, Melville embarked upon three lecture tours, where he spoke mainly on Roman statuary and sightseeing in Rome. These lectures mocked the pseudo-intellectualism of lyceum culture. His words though were ignored by contemporary audiences.

In the 1860's he wrote many poems, many based on the Civil War. But there was no publisher for him and no audience.

In 1866, Melville's wife and her relatives used their influence to obtain a position for him as customs inspector for the City of New York, With his writings almost ignored they moved to New York where Melville joined the New York Customs house and worked there for the next 19 years.

For Melville his early promise and great talents seemed to be getting him nowhere in literary terms. Despite periods of drinking, depression and other ails Elizabeth stood by her husband despite calls from other family members and the marriage held together.

In 1876 he was at last able to publish privately his 16,000 line epic poem Clarel, in which a young American student of divinity travels to Jerusalem to renew his faith. It was to no avail. The book had an initial printing of 350 copies, but sales failed miserably, and the unsold copies were burned when Melville was unable to afford to buy them at cost.

On December 31st, 1885 Melville was at last able to retire. His wife had inherited several small legacies and with her astute ways it was enough to provide them with a reasonable income and Melville had enough to buy further precious books and supplies.

In these last few years Melville finished two poetry collections which were printed privately, although only 25 copies of each; John Marr and Other Sailors (1888) and Timoleon (1891).

Herman Melville, novelist, poet, short story writer and essayist, died at his home on September 28rh 1891 from cardiovascular disease.

He was interred in the Woodlawn Cemetery in The Bronx, New York City.

He was the first writer to have his works collected and published by the Library of America.

Herman Melville – A Concise Bibliography

Novels, Short Stories & Poetry

Typee: A Peep at Polynesian Life (1846)
Omoo: A Narrative of Adventures in the South Seas (1847)
Mardi: And a Voyage Thither (1849)
Redburn: His First Voyage (1849)
White-Jacket; or, The World in a Man-of-War (1850)
Moby-Dick; or, The Whale (1851)
Pierre: or, The Ambiguities (1852)
Isle of the Cross (1853 unpublished, and now lost)
Cock-A-doodle-Doo (Short story) (1852)
Bartleby, the Scrivener (Short story) (1853)
The Encantadas, or Enchanted Isles (Short story) (1854)
Poor Man's Pudding and Rich Man's Crumbs (Short story) (1854)
The Happy Failure (Short story) (1854)
The Lightning-Rod Man (Short story) (1854)
The Fiddler (Short story) (1854)
Benito Cereno (1855)
Israel Potter: His Fifty Years of Exile (1855)
The Paradise of Batchelors and the Tartarus of Maids (Short story) (1855)
The Bell-Tower (Short story) (1855)
Jimmy Rose (Short story) (1855)
The Gees (Short story) (1856)
I and My Chimney (Short story) (1856)
The Apple-Tree Story (Short story) (1856)
The Confidence-Man: His Masquerade (1857)
The Piazza (Short story) (1856)
Battle-Pieces and Aspects of the War (Poetry) (1866)
Clarel: A Poem and Pilgrimage in the Holy Land (Epic poem) (1876)
John Marr and Other Sailors (Poetry) (1888)
Timoleon (Poetry) (1891)
Billy Budd, Sailor (An Inside Narrative) (1891 unfinished, published posthumously in 1924)

Essays

Fragments from a Writing Desk, No. 1 (May 4, 1839)
Fragments from a Writing Desk, No. 2 (May 18, 1839)
Etchings of a Whaling Cruise (1847)
Authentic Anecdotes of 'Old Zack" (July 24 to September 11, 1847)
Mr Parkman's Tour (March 31, 1849)
Cooper's New Novel (April 28, 1849)
A Thought on Book-Binding (March 16, 1850)
Hawthorne and His Mosses (August 17 and August 24, 1850)

www.ingramcontent.com/pod-product-compliance
Lightning Source LLC
Chambersburg PA
CBHW060118050426
42448CB00010B/1929